Frank M. Chapman

Visitors' Guide to the Local Collection of Birds

in the American Museum of Natural History, New York City. With an annotated list of the birds known to occur within fifty miles of New York City

Frank M. Chapman

Visitors' Guide to the Local Collection of Birds
in the American Museum of Natural History, New York City. With an annotated list of the birds known to occur within fifty miles of New York City

ISBN/EAN: 9783337218256

Printed in Europe, USA, Canada, Australia, Japan

Cover: Foto ©Andreas Hilbeck / pixelio.de

More available books at **www.hansebooks.com**

Visitors' Guide

to the

Collection ■ Birds

Found within Fifty Miles of New York City

Visitors' Guide

TO THE

Local Collection of Birds

IN THE

American Museum of Natural History

NEW YORK CITY.

WITH

AN ANNOTATED LIST
OF THE
BIRDS KNOWN TO OCCUR WITHIN FIFTY MILES
OF NEW YORK CITY

BY

FRANK M. CHAPMAN, Assistant Curator
Department of Mammalogy and Ornithology

NEW YORK:
PRINTED FOR THE MUSEUM
1894

INTRODUCTION.

The collection this Guide is intended to accompany has been formed especially to aid students in identifying the birds found in the vicinity of New York City. It occupies Cases S and T, in the north wing, at the southwest corner of the gallery devoted to North American birds. With a few exceptions all the specimens contained in it were collected within 50 miles of New York City. The species which we have as yet been unable to secure within these limits are represented temporarily by specimens from the North American collection. The collection of Water Birds is for the present restricted to summer resident species. So large a proportion of North American Water Birds are found near New York City, that a local collection of them would to a great extent duplicate the North American collection displayed on the opposite side of the gallery. Species of accidental occurrence, or those which have been found in this vicinity but once or twice, are also excluded from the collection. Their presence would only tend to confuse the student and be apt to give him an erroneous idea of the bird's range.

The birds are labeled in accordance with the system of nomenclature adopted by the American Ornithologists' Union. The number preceding the name of each species is its permanent number in the Union's 'Check-List' of North American birds. In the Guide this number *follows* the name of the species. The birds are placed in the cases in a continuous numerical series and any desired specimen may thus be readily found by its number. As a matter of local interest an asterisk (*) has been placed before those species which have been observed in Central Park.

In the alcove between Cases B and C, in the main bird-hall, will be found a local collection of the nests and eggs of the birds which breed within 50 miles of New York City. It is labeled on the same plan as the local collection of birds.

In order that the student may know the names of all the birds which have been found here, the following annotated list of the species known to occur within a radius of 50 miles of New York City is presented. It is based on information derived for the most part from three sources: (1) previously published records; (2) the author's notes covering a period of ten years' intermittent observation, mainly at Englewood, N. J.; (3) information received from Mr. William Dutcher. For the past 15 years Mr. Dutcher has made a specialty of the study of Long Island birds and has brought together a vast amount of data concerning them. He has kindly revised the manuscript of this Guide, thereby adding largely to its accuracy.

The excellent cuts with which this Guide is illustrated are from Coues's 'Key to North American Birds.' For their use the Museum is indebted to Messrs. Estes and Lauriat the publishers of that work. The full-page plates were used in Dr. Shufeldt's recent memoir on 'Scientific Taxidermy'. They are printed from electrotypes kindly furnished us by the United States National Museum.

The region embraced within our limits possesses natural advantages calculated to attract a great number of birds. Our sea-coast, with its sandy beaches and shallow bays; our rivers, creeks and ponds, with their surrounding grassy marshes; our wooded hillsides and valleys; our rolling uplands and fertile meadows, offer haunts suited to the wants of most birds. Again, our coast-line and the Hudson River Valley form natural highways of migration regularly followed by birds in their journeys to and from their summer homes.

But the exceptional abundance of birds in this vicinity is not due alone to the varied character of the country, or to the fact that twice each year streams of migrants pass along our coasts and through our valleys. There are certain causes which tend to limit the ranges of animals. Chief among these is temperature. A study of the ranges or habitats of animals and plants shows that the boundaries of the habitats of many species coincide with one another and also to a greater or less extent with lines of equal temperature. The ranges of these species being thus governed by natural causes are taken as indices of the limits of faunas or natural life-areas. The lines between these faunas cannot, of course, be sharply drawn. The change from one to another is gradual, and thus between the two a neutral strip exists in which will be found species characteristic of each. Just such a condition is found in this vicinity; the northern boundary of the Carolinian Fauna over-lapping the southern boundary of the Alleghanian Fauna in the valleys of the Delaware, Hudson, and Connecticut. In other words, we have here on the one hand a number of birds which are found no farther north, and on the other certain species which are found no farther south. That is, in the breeding season; for among birds only the nesting ranges are of value in determining the boundaries of faunas.

The southern limit of the Carolinian Fauna on the Atlantic Coast is near Norfolk, Virginia; its northern limit, on the coast, as said above, is in the vicinity of New York City. To be more exact, a careful study of the nesting ranges of certain species shows that the most northern points at which they are regularly found is Port Jervis in the Delaware Valley, Fishkill in the Hudson River Valley, and Portland in the Connecticut River Valley. These localities then may be considered as defining the northern limits of the Carolinian Fauna in the valleys in which they are placed. In the more elevated country between these points it is doubtful if the limits of the fauna reach quite as far north, for river valleys, both because they offer a natural pathway for the extension of a bird's range, and because of the higher temperature prevailing in them, tend to carry northward the boundaries of faunas. Eastward, along the Connecticut shore, the Carolinian Fauna may reach the mouth of the Thames. Long Island, although farther south, belongs for the most part in the Alleghanian rather than the Carolinian Fauna. Numbers of species common and even abundant in the Lower Hudson Valley are exceedingly rare on Long Island, especially on the southern shore. But along the northern shore, or older part of the island, where deciduous trees abound, there is an evident trace of the Carolinian Fauna shown by the regular occurrence of the Blue-winged Warbler and Acadian Flycatcher.

The following Carolinian birds are found every summer within 50 miles of New York City, and all but two or three are known to nest regularly here. Their occurrence northward beyond these limits is rare and irregular, and but two or three have been known to nest north of the 50 mile line.

Snowy Heron.
Clapper Rail.
King Rail.
Turkey Vulture.
Barn Owl.
Acadian Flycatcher.
Fish Crow.
Cardinal.
Rough-winged Swallow.

Worm-eating Warbler.
Blue-winged Warbler.
Louisiana Water-Thrush.
Kentucky Warbler.
Hooded Warbler.
Mockingbird.
Carolina Wren.
Tufted Titmouse.
Carolina Chickadee.

Blue-gray Gnatcatcher.

Not more than five of these, however, advance *regularly* to the northern limits of the Fauna. The southern limits of the Alleghanian Fauna on the coast is less clearly defined. It includes, however, Long Island and northern New Jersey. Its boundaries are in a measure defined by the presence in the breeding season of the following species, none of which are known to nest south of this vicinity at sea-level.

Carolina Rail.
Purple Finch.
Golden-winged Warbler.

Nashville Warbler.
Chestnut-sided Warbler.
Black-throated Green Warbler.

Thus it will be seen that while the region south of our district has the Carolinian species mentioned, and the region to the northward has the Alleghanian species just given, we, in this intermediate or neutral strip, have both Carolinian and Alleghanian species.

It is evident therefore that from an ornithological standpoint we are most favorably situated, and a comparison of the number of birds found within our limits with the numbers recorded from other districts shows that the causes mentioned have been effective in giving us an unusually rich avifauna. Due allowance must of course be made for the much greater area included in all but one of the regions used in comparison.

Recorded from within 50 Miles of New York City   348
"   "   District Columbia (Richmond, MS.)   281
"   "   Ontario, Canada, (McIlwraith)   .   316
*   "   Massachusetts (Allen)   .   .   . 349
"   "   Illinois (Ridgway)   352
"   "   Indiana (Butler)   . 305
"   "   Michigan (Cook)   332
"   "   Kansas (Goss)   343

During the course of a year the bird-life of our vicinity is subject to great changes. Some birds are always with us, some come for the summer, others pass us in the spring and fall in traveling to and from their more northern homes, and others still come only in the winter. Our birds may thus be arranged, according to the season when they are present, in several more or less well defined groups, for which the following names seem most applicable.

I. Permanent Residents.—This class includes species which are with us throughout the year. It does not follow that the same individuals pass the entire year here. Comparatively few of the species in this group are permanent residents in the strict sense of the term. The Bob-white, Ruffed Grouse, and several of the Owls are doubtless literally permanent residents, that is, the same individuals pass their lives in one restricted locality. But it is not probable that the Bluebirds, for example, found here during the winter are the same birds which nested with us in the summer. Doubtless our winter Bluebirds passed the summer farther north, while our summer Bluebirds winter farther south. Still as a species the Bluebird is a permanent resident.

LIST OF PERMANENT RESIDENTS.

Bob-white.
Ruffed grouse.
Marsh Hawk.
Sharp-shinned Hawk.
Cooper's Hawk.
Red-tailed Hawk.
Red-shouldered Hawk.
Broad-winged Hawk.
Bald Eagle.
Duck Hawk.
Sparrow Hawk.
Long-eared Owl.
Barred Owl.
Screech Owl.
Great Horned Owl.
Hairy Woodpecker.
Downy Woodpecker.
Flicker.
Prairie Horned Lark.
Blue Jay.
American Crow.
Fish Crow.
Starling.
Meadowlark.
House Sparrow.
Purple Finch.
American Goldfinch.
European Goldfinch.
Song Sparrow.
Swamp Sparrow.
Cardinal.
Cedar Waxwing.
Carolina Wren.
White-breasted Nuthatch.
Tufted Titmouse.
Chickadee.
Robin.
Bluebird.

II. Summer Residents.—Summer residents, as the name implies, are birds found here during the summer. They may, however, arrive early in March and remain until December, as do the Blackbirds and Woodcock, or they may not come until May and leave us in August. Summer residents then, are birds which come to us at varying times in the spring and after nesting here, return to their more southern winter resorts in the fall.

LIST OF SUMMER RESIDENTS.

Pied-billed Grebe.
Laughing Gull.
Common Tern.
Roseate Tern.
Black Duck.
Wood Duck.
American Bittern.
Least Bittern.
Great Blue Heron.
Snowy Heron.
Green Heron.
Black-crowned Night Heron.
King Rail.
Clapper Rail.
Virginia Rail.
Sora.
? Yellow Rail.
Black Rail.
Woodcock.
Bartramian Sandpiper.
Spotted Sandpiper.
Kildeer.
Piping Plover.
Mourning Dove.
Osprey.
Barn Owl.
Yellow-billed Cuckoo.
Black-billed Cuckoo.
Belted Kingfisher.
Red-headed Woodpecker.
Whip-poor-will.
Nighthawk.
Chimney Swift.
Ruby-throated Hummingbird.
Kingbird.
Crested Flycatcher.
Phœbe.
Wood Pewee.
Acadian Flycatcher.
Least Flycatcher.
Bobolink.
Cowbird.
Red-winged Blackbird.
Orchard Oriole.
Baltimore Oriole.
Purple Grackle.

Vesper Sparrow.
Savanna Sparrow.
Grasshopper Sparrow.
Henslow's Sparrow.
Sharp-tailed Sparrow.
Seaside Sparrow.
Chipping Sparrow.
Field Sparrow.
Towhee.
Rose-breasted Grosbeak.
Indigo Bunting.
Scarlet Tanager.
Purple Martin.
Cliff Swallow.
Barn Swallow.
Tree Swallow.
Bank Swallow.
Rough-winged Swallow.
Red-eyed Vireo.
Warbling Vireo.
Yellow-throated Vireo.
White-eyed Vireo.
Black and White Warbler.
Worm-eating Warbler.
Blue-winged Warbler.
Golden-winged Warbler.
Parula Warbler.
Yellow Warbler.
Chestnut-sided Warbler.
Pine Warbler.
Prairie Warbler.
Ovenbird.
Louisiana Water-Thrush.
Kentucky Warbler.
Maryland Yellow-throat.
Yellow-breasted Chat.
Hooded Warbler.
Redstart.
Mockingbird.
Catbird.
Brown Thrasher.
House Wren.
Short-billed Marsh Wren.
Long-billed Marsh Wren.
Wood Thrush.
Wilson's Thrush.

III. Summer Visitants.—Comparatively few birds fall into this group. As a rule the northern limit of their breeding range is not far south of our southern boundaries and they sometimes visit us in small numbers after their breeding season is over. In this group may also be placed the Shearwaters and Petrels, some of which are known to nest in the Antarctic Regions during our winter. In the spring they migrate northward and pass the summer off our coasts.

LIST OF SUMMER VISITANTS.

Gull-billed Tern.
Royal Tern.
Forster's Tern.
Sooty Tern.
Black Skimmer.
Greater Shearwater.
Audubon's Shearwater.
Sooty Shearwater.
Wilson's Petrel.
American Egret.
Little Blue Heron.
Wilson's Plover.
Oyster-catcher.
Turkey Vulture.
Red-bellied Woodpecker.
Summer Tanager.
Carolina Chickadee.
Blue-gray Gnatcatcher.

IV. Winter Residents.—Winter residents, like summer residents, may arrive long before and remain long after the season which gives them their name. Our Junco, or Snowbird, for example, comes from the north in September and remains until April, but is a typical winter resident. That is, it arrives in the fall and after passing the entire winter with us returns to its more northern summer home in the spring.

LIST OF WINTER RESIDENTS.

Holbœll's Grebe.
Horned Grebe.
Loon.
Red-throated Loon
Razor-billed Auk.
Kittiwake Gull.
Glaucous Gull.
Great Black-backed Gull.
Herring Gull.
Ring-billed Gull.
Green-winged Teal.
American Golden-eye.
Buffle-head.
Old-squaw.
King Eider.
American Scoter.
White-winged Scoter
Surf Scoter.
Purple Sandpiper.
Rough-legged Hawk.
Saw-whet Owl.
Horned Lark.
American Crossbill.
Redpoll.
Pine Siskin.
Snowflake.
Lapland Longspur.
Ipswich Sparrow.
White-throated Sparrow.
Tree Sparrow.
Junco.
Northern Shrike.
Winter Wren.
Brown Creeper.
Canadian Nuthatch.
Golden-crowned Kinglet.

V. Winter Visitants.—Winter visitants are birds which may or may not visit us during the winter. As a rule their presence depends upon the severity of the winter. An unusually severe season sometimes forces boreal birds southward and they then may be found in numbers south of the limits of their regular winter homes.

LIST OF WINTER VISITANTS.

Puffin.
Black Guillemot.
Brünnich's Murre.
Dovekie.
Cormorant.
Harlequin Duck.
American Eider.
Goshawk.

Black Gyrfalcon?
Hawk Owl.
Snowy Owl.
Evening Grosbeak.
Pine Grosbeak.
White-winged Crossbill.
Holbœll's Redpoll.
Bohemian Waxwing.

VI. Regular Transient Visitants.—The birds of this class are found here only during the migrations. Their summer homes are north of us, their winter homes are south of us, and we see them only when they pass northward on their spring migration and southward on their fall migration.

LIST OF REGULAR TRANSIENT VISITANTS.

Pomarine Jaeger.
Parasitic Jaeger.
Long-tailed Jaeger.
Bonaparte's Gull.
Caspian Tern.
Cory's Shearwater.
Leach's Petrel.
Gannet.
Double-crested Cormorant.
Red-breasted Merganser.
Hooded Merganser.
Blue-winged Teal.
Pintail.
Red-head.
American Scaup Duck.
Lesser Scaup Duck.
Ruddy Duck.
Canada Goose.
Brant.
Florida Gallinule.
Coot.
Red Phalarope.
Northern Phalarope.
Wilson's Snipe.

Dowitcher.
Long-billed Dowitcher.
Stilt Sandpiper.
Knot.
Pectoral Sandpiper.
White-rumped Sandpiper.
Least Sandpiper.
Red-backed Sandpiper.
Semipalmated Sandpiper.
Western Sandpiper.
Sanderling.
Greater Yellow-legs.
Yellow-legs.
Solitary Sandpiper.
Willet.
Hudsonian Curlew.
Eskimo Curlew.
Black-bellied Plover.
Golden Plover.
Semipalmated Plover.
Turnstone.
Pigeon Hawk.
Short-eared Owl.
Yellow-bellied Woodpecker.

Olive-sided Flycatcher.
Yellow-bellied Flycatcher.
Traill's Flycatcher.
Rusty Blackbird.
Bronzed Grackle.
Nelson's Sharp-tailed Sparrow.
Acadian Sharp-tailed Sparrow.
White-crowned Sparrow.
Lincoln's Sparrow.
Fox Sparrow.
Philadelphia Vireo.
Blue-headed Vireo.
Nashville Warbler.
Tennessee Warbler.
Cape May Warbler.
Black-throated Blue Warbler.
Myrtle Warbler.
Magnolia Warbler.
Bay-breasted Warbler.
Black-poll Warbler.
Blackburnian Warbler.
Black-throated Green Warbler.
Yellow Palm Warbler.
Water-Thrush.
Connecticut Warbler.
Mourning Warbler.
Wilson's Warbler.
Canadian Warbler.
Titlark.
Ruby-crowned Kinglet.
Gray-cheeked Thrush.
Bicknell's Thrush.
Swainson's Thrush.
Hermit Thrush.

VII. Irregular Transient Visitants.—These birds occur irregularly during the migrations. With certain exceptions they are birds of the interior and breed in the northern United States and British Provinces. Their regular line of migration is down the Mississippi Valley, and their occurrence on the Atlantic coast is more or less infrequent. Here are also included species formerly common near New York but now practically extinct within our limits, where, however, they are sometimes found.

LIST OF IRREGULAR TRANSIENT VISITANTS.

Least Tern.
Black Tern.
Mallard.
Gadwall.
American Widgeon.
Shoveller.
Canvas-back.
Ring-necked Duck.
Greater Snow Goose.
Blue Goose.
American White-fronted Goose.
Hutchins's Goose.
Black Brant.
Whistling Swan.
Wilson's Phalarope.
American Avocet.
Baird's Sandpiper.
Marbled Godwit.
Hudsonian Godwit.
Buff-breasted Sandpiper.
Long-billed Curlew.
Belted Piping Plover.
Passenger Pigeon.
Golden Eagle.
Pileated Woodpecker.
Raven.
Loggerhead Shrike.
Orange-crowned Warbler.
Palm Warbler.
Grinnell's Water-Thrush.

VIII. Accidental Visitants.—The homes of the birds included in this class are so far removed from our boundaries that their presence here at any time can be considered only as purely accidental. In most cases it is doubtless due to the agency of storms or high winds which drive migrating birds from their course. One-fourth the number given below are Old World birds, and about one-half the total number have been found here but once.

LIST OF ACCIDENTAL VISITANTS.

Black-throated Loon.
Little Gull.
Sabine's Gull.
Fulmar.
Booby.
White Pelican.
Brown Pelican.
European Widgeon.
European Green-winged Teal.
Rufous-crested Duck.
Barnacle Goose.
White Ibis.
Glossy Ibis.
Yellow-crowned Night Heron.
Corn Crake.
Purple Gallinule.
Black-necked Stilt.
European Woodcock.
Curlew Sandpiper.

Ruff.
Lapwing.
Ground Dove.
Black Vulture.
Swallow-tailed Kite.
Swainson's Hawk.
White Gyrfalcon.
Great Gray Owl.
Red-cockaded Woodpecker.
Arkansas Kingbird.
Chestnut-collared Longspur.
Lark Sparrow.
Blue Grosbeak.
Painted Bunting.
Dickcissel.
Louisiana Tanager.
Prothonotary Warbler.
Cerulean Warbler.
Yellow-throated Warbler.

Wheatear.

SUMMARY.

Permanent Residents	35
Summer Residents	92
Summer Visitants	18
Winter Residents	36
Winter Visitants	16
Regular Transient Visitants	82
Irregular Transient Visitants	30
Accidental Visitants	39
Total.	348

LIST OF BIRDS FOUND WITHIN FIFTY MILES OF NEW YORK CITY.

Order PYGOPODES. Diving Birds.

Family PODICIPIDÆ.—GREBES.

1. Colymbus holbœllii (*Reinh.*). HOLBŒLL'S GREBE. (2.)—Breeds from Manitoba northward; in winter migrates southward as far as South Carolina. With us it is a rather uncommon spring and fall migrant and less common winter resident

2. Colymbus auritus (*Linn.*). HORNED GREBE. (3.)—Breeds from the northern United States northward and winters southward to Florida. It is here a common spring and fall migrant and not uncommon winter resident.

*3. Podilymbus podiceps (*Linn.*). PIED-BILLED GREBE; DIE-DAPPER; DABCHICK; HELL-DIVER. (6.)—Ranges from the Argentine Republic northward to Great Slave Lake, breeding locally throughout its range. In the vicinity of New York it occurs chiefly as a migrant. In northern New Jersey and the Lower Hudson Valley it is common but on Long Island is of "comparatively rare and infrequent occurrence" (*Dutcher*, MS.). It breeds here rarely and during favorable seasons a few pass the winter. (See Group, main floor, opposite case C.)

Family URINATORIDÆ.—LOONS.

4. Urinator imber (*Gunn.*) LOON. (7.)—"Breeds from about latitude 42° to within the Arctic Circle. During the winter it is found.... from Maine to Florida." In this locality the Loon is a common migrant and less common winter resident. (See Group, main floor, opposite case B)

FIG. 1. LOON.

5. Urinator arcticus (*Linn.*). BLACK-THROATED LOON. (9.)—Breeds in the far north, migrating southward to Southern Canada. The only record of its occurrence near New York is based on an adult male taken April 29, 1893, between Sands Point and Execution Lighthouse, L. I. (*Dutcher*, Auk, X, 1893, p. 265).

6. Urinator lumme (*Gunn*). RED-THROATED LOON. (11.)—Breeds from New Brunswick northward; in winter migrates irregularly southward, occasionally to South Carolina. About New York it is a not uncommon winter resident but is more frequently found during the migrations.

Family ALCIDÆ.—AUKS, MURRES, and PUFFINS.

7. Fratercula arctica (*Linn*). PUFFIN. (13.)—Breeds from the Bay of Fundy northward; in winter migrates southward, coming rarely as far as Long Island. There is but one recent record of its occurrence, viz., December 15, 1882, Centre Moriches, L. I. (*Dutcher*, Auk, V, 1888, p. 171).

8. Cepphus grylle (*Linn.*). BLACK GUILLEMOT. (27.)—Breeds from the Bay of Fundy northward; in winter migrates southward, regularly to Massachusetts. It has been found but once in Connecticut (Stony Creek, Dec. 1887.—*Sage*, Auk, VII, 1890, p. 283), and the only Long Island record, given by Lawrence, is apparently based on a specimen in the Lawrence Collection labeled "Long Island".

9. Uria lomvia (*Linn.*). BRÜNNICH'S MURRE. (31.)—Breeds from the Magdalen Islands northward; in winter migrates southward as far as New Jersey. On the western end of Long Island it is as a rule uncommon; at the eastern end it occurs more frequently but is irregular (*Dutcher*, Auk, II, 1885, p. 38). During some seasons, however, they become common in our waters (*Averill*, Auk, VIII, 1891, p. 307). Giraud's record of "*Uria troile*" doubtless refers to this species. Specimens in the Lawrence Collection orginally labeled "*U. troile*" are *U. lomvia*.

10. Alca torda (*Linn.*). RAZOR-BILLED AUK. (32.)—Breeds from the Magdalen Islands northward; in winter migrates southward, regularly to Long Island, and rarely to Virginia and North Carolina.

11. Alle alle (*Linn.*). DOVEKIE. (34.)—A species of the far north, migrating southward in winter, more or less regularly to New Jersey. With us its numbers vary during different winters. It is considered by Dutcher to be generally a rare bird on Long Island (Abst. Linn. Soc. No. 4, 1892, p. 6), but is given by Scott as a regular winter visitant on the New Jersey coast (Bull. Nutt. Orn. Club, IV, 1879, p. 228).

Order LONGIPENNES. Long-winged Swimmers.

Family STERCORARIIDÆ.—SKUAS AND JAEGERS.

12. Stercorarius pomarinus (*Temm.*). POMARINE JAEGER. (36.)—Passes the nesting season chiefly within the Arctic Circle, and migrates southward from July to late October during which period it is sometimes not uncommon off our coast; its presence depending largely on the abundance of the small fish on which it feeds (*Baird*, Auk, IV, 1887, p. 71).

13. Stercorarius parasiticus (*Linn.*). PARASITIC JAEGER. (37.)—Breeds in the Barren Grounds of Arctic America and in southern Greenland; migrates southward to the Great Lakes, and along the Atlantic coast to South America; winters from the Middle States southward. It occurs off the coast in this vicinity as a regular migrant with the preceding species.

14. Stercorarius longicaudus *Vieill.* LONG-TAILED JAEGER. (38.—Breeds in about the same region as the preceding and migrates southward to the Great Lakes and Gulf of Mexico. During its migrations it is sometimes not uncommon off our coast.

Family LARIDÆ —GULLS AND TERNS.

15. Rissa tridactyla (*Linn.*). KITTIWAKE GULL. (40.)—Breeds from the Gulf of St. Lawrence northward, and winters on the Great Lakes, and along the Atlantic coast as far south as Massachusetts, occasionally reaching Virginia. With us it is a common late fall transient visitant and a comparatively rare winter resident, occuring generally some distance off-shore (*Dutcher*, MS.).

16. Larus glaucus *Brünn.* GLAUCOUS GULL; BURGOMASTER (42.)—Breeds from Labrador northward; found in winter as far south as Long Island. Several specimens have been killed on the Lower Hudson River, and on Long Island it is found regularly in small numbers (*Dutcher*, MS.).

17. Larus marinus *Linn.* GREAT BLACK-BACKED GULL. (47.) —Breeds from the Bay of Fundy northward, and migrates southward in the winter to the Great Lakes and Virginia. In this vicinity it is a regular, but not common, winter resident.

*__18. Larus argentatus smithsonianus__ *Coues.* HERRING GULL. (51a.)—"North America generally, breeding on the Atlantic coast from Maine northward"; winters from Nova Scotia to Cuba.

This is the common winter Gull of our harbor and coast. It arrives from the north in September, and is abundant until April. The adults are pearl gray; the immature birds, or young born the previous summer, are grayish brown.

19. Larus delawarensis *Ord.* RING-BILLED GULL. (54.)—Breeds from Newfoundland northward, and in the interior, where it is more common, from Southern Minnesota northward; winters south to Cuba and Mexico. It is here a rather uncommon spring and fall migrant and winter resident (*Dutcher*, MS.).

20. Larus atricilla *Linn.* LAUGHING GULL. (58.)—Breeds from Florida to Maine, and winters from South Carolina to Brazil. It was formerly a common summer resident on Long Island, but now is known to nest only on Great South Bay, where it is rare. (See Group, main floor, opp. case G.)

21. Larus philadelphia (*Ord*). BONAPARTE'S GULL. (60.)—Breeds in the interior from Manitoba northward (apparently no record of its breeding on the Atlantic coast), and migrates southward to the Gulf of Mexico. It is found here as a regular spring and fall migrant, and is sometimes seen in winter.

22. Larus minutus *Pall.* LITTLE GULL. (60.1)—This is a European species; the only satisfactory record of its occurrence in North America is that of an immature bird taken on Fire Island, Long Island, September 15, 1887 (*Dutcher*, Auk, V, 1888, p. 172).

23. Xema sabinii (*Sab.*). SABINE'S GULL. (62.)—A circumpolar species, breeding in the Far North and rarely coming as far south as the northern United States. Giraud records a specimen shot at Raynor South, Long Island, "July, 1837".

24. Gelochelidon nilotica (*Hasselq.*). GULL-BILLED TERN. (63.)—A southern species, breeding as far north as southern New Jersey, and wandering occasionally to Maine. There are several Long Island records, the most recent being two specimens taken at South Oyster Bay, July 4, 1882 (*Dutcher*, Auk, I, 1884, p. 34), and one shot from a flock of five on Shinnecock Bay, July 8, 1884 (*Dutcher*, Auk, II, 1885, p. 38).

25. Sterna tschegrava *Lepech.* CASPIAN TERN. (64.)—Breeds locally from Texas to Great Slave Lake. In this vicinity it is found as a rather uncommon migrant.

26. Sterna maxima *Bodd.* ROYAL TERN. (65.)—A southern species, breeding as far north as Virginia, and occasionally wandering northward to Massachusetts. There is but one known instance of its occurrence on Long Island, — a specimen taken at Raynor South, August 27, 1831, by J. F. Ward (Am. Mus. No. 46,008, Lawrence Coll.).

27. Sterna forsteri *Nutt.* FORSTER'S TERN. (64.)—More common in the interior than on the Atlantic coast, where it is not known to breed north of Virginia. It wanders irregularly northward, and is sometimes found in this vicinity.

28. Sterna hirundo *Linn.* COMMON TERN; SEA SWALLOW. (70.)—Inhabits the greater part of the Northern Hemisphere; in North America breeds locally from the Arctic Regions to the Gulf of Mexico. This was formerly an abundant bird along our coasts, but the relentless persecutions of millinery collectors have so reduced its numbers that it is now found in only a few isolated localities. Not many years ago it bred more or less commonly all along the Long Island coast, but almost the only surviving colony (numbering about 1000 pairs) inhabits Big Gull Island. Even in this remote locality it is constantly persecuted by nest-robbing fishermen and self-styled oölogists, who will doubtless soon effect its complete extinction. (Since the above was written, through the efforts of a number of bird-lovers who raised a sum of money for the purpose, permission has been obtained from the Lighthouse Board to have the lightkeeper on Little Gull Island appointed a special game-keeper whose duty it shall be to protect the Terns on Big Gull Island.)

FIG. 2. TERN.

29. **Sterna dougalli** *Montag*. ROSEATE TERN. (72.)—"Temperate and tropical regions". In North America formerly breeding along the Atlantic coast northward irregularly to Maine; now rare north of southern New Jersey. A few pairs live on Big Gull Island with the colony of Common Terns above mentioned.

The Arctic Tern (*Sterna paradisæa*) is included by Lawrence without remark. I know of no record of its occurrence near New York City, and Mr. Dutcher has but one specimen from Long Island, a male taken on Ram Island Shoals, July 1, 1884.

30. **Sterna antillarum** (*Less.*). LEAST TERN. (74 —Northern South America, northward to California, Dakota, and Massachusetts, breeding locally throughout its range. Formerly a common summer resident in suitable places on the coasts in this vicinity, but now occurs only as a rare migrant.

31. **Sterna fuliginosa** *Gmel*. SOOTY TERN. (75.)—A southern species, not breeding north of North Carolina, but occasionally straying farther up the coast. It has been recorded from Lake Ronkonkoma, L. I. (*Dutcher*, Auk, III, 1886, p. 433), and Highland Falls, N. Y. (*Mearns*, Bull. Essex. Inst., XII, 1879, 87).

32. Hydrochelidon nigra surinamensis (*Gmel.*). BLACK TERN. (77.)—A species of the interior, breeding from Kansas and Illinois to Alaska. Occurs on the Atlantic coast as an irregular migrant, sometimes in considerable numbers.

Family RYNCHOPIDÆ.—SKIMMERS.

33. Rynchops nigra *Linn.* BLACK SKIMMER. (80.)—A southern species, not breeding north of southern New Jersey, but occasionally wandering up the coast after the breeding season. There are a number of records of its occurence during the summer on Long Island.

Order TUBINARES. Tube-nosed Swimmers.

Family PROCELLARIIDÆ—FULMARS AND SHEARWATERS.

34. Fulmarus glacialis (*Linn.*). FULMAR. (86.)—An Arctic species which sometimes wanders southward to Massachusetts. One was found in an exhausted condition at Ridgewood, New Jersey, December, 1892, after a storm (*Hales*, Orn. and Oöl., XVII, 1892, p. 39).

35. Puffinus borealis *Cory.* CORY'S SHEARWATER. (88.)—A pelagic species, sometimes not uncommon off our coasts from August to November. It has been recorded from Amagansett, Long Island (*Dutcher*, Auk, V, 1888, p. 5), to Cape Cod, Massachusetts, but doubtless occurs along our coast to the southward.

36. Puffinus major *Faber.* GREATER SHEARWATER. (89.)—A pelagic species, found on the Atlantic Ocean from Cape Horn to Greenland. Its breeding place is unknown. It appears off our coasts in early June, and is irregularly common until November.

37. Puffinus auduboni *Finsch.* AUDUBON'S SHEARWATER. (92.)—A southern species, breeding in the Bahamas and Bermudas, and rarely wandering northward to Long Island (*Dutcher*, Auk, V, 1888, p. 173).

38. Puffinus stricklandi *Ridgw.* SOOTY SHEARWATER. (94.)—Known from the North Atlantic southward to South Carolina. It is found off our coasts associated with the Greater Shearwater, but is much less common.

The Stormy Petrel (*Procellaria pelagica*) is included by Lawrence in his "Catalogue of Birds Observed on New York Island" etc., but the record is not accompanied by data, nor is there a specimen of the bird from this vicinity in the Lawrence Collection.

39. Oceanodroma leucorhoa (*Vieill.*). LEACH'S PETREL. (106.)—Breeds from Maine northward, and in the winter ranges southward to Virginia. It is rather uncommon in this vicinity.

40. Oceanites oceanicus (*Kuhl*). WILSON'S PETREL. (109.)—Nests in the islands of the Southern Seas (Kerguelen Island) in January and February, and migrates northward after the breeding season, reaching the waters off our coasts in May and remaining until late September.

FIG. 3. PETREL.

Order STEGANOPODES. Totipalmate Swimmers.

Family SULIDÆ.—GANNETS.

41. Sula sula (*Linn.*). BOOBY. (115.)—Coasts and islands of tropical and sub-tropical America, north of Georgia. Accidental on Moriches Bay, Long Island (*Dutcher*, Auk, X, 1893, p. 270).

42. Sula bassana (*Linn.*). GANNET. (117.)—Nests from Nova Scotia northward, and winters as far south as the Gulf of Mexico. It occurs here as a spring and fall migrant.

Family PHALACROCORACIDÆ.—CORMORANTS.

43. Phalacrocorax carbo (*Linn.*). CORMORANT. (119.)—Breeds from Nova Scotia northward, and winters as far south as the Carolinas. It is not common south of Maine, and is rare in this vicinity.

44. Phalacrocorax dilophus (*Sw. & Rich.*). DOUBLE-CRESTED CORMORANT. (120.)—Breeds from Dakota, Minnesota, and the Bay of Fundy northward, and winters from Illinois and Virginia southward. It is here a common spring and fall migrant.

Family PELECANIDÆ.—PELICANS.

45. Pelecanus erythrorhynchos *Gmel.* WHITE PELICAN. (125.)—North America; now rare or accidental on the Atlantic coast; breeds from southern Minnesota northward and winters along the Gulf coasts. Two specimens have been taken in this vicinity, one at Carnarsie Bay, L. I. (*Dutcher*, Auk, X, 1893, p. 270), the other, a male, at Roslyn, May 11, 1885 (Forest and Stream, XXIV, 1885, p. 328).

46. Pelecanus fuscus *Linn.* BROWN PELICAN. (126.)—Breeds as far north as South Carolina, and occasionally strays up the coast as far as Massachusetts. DeKay records a specimen from Sandy Hook.

Order ANSERES. Lamellirostral Swimmers.

Family ANATIDÆ.—DUCKS, GEESE, AND SWANS.

47. Merganser americanus (*Cass.*). AMERICAN MERGANSER; SHELLDRAKE. (129.)—Breeds from southern New Brunswick northward, and winters from the southern limit of its breeding range southward to the Carolinas. In this vicinity it is not common from November to April.

48. Merganser serrator (*Linn.*). RED-BREASTED MERGANSER; SHELLDRAKE. (130.)—Breeds from New Brunswick northward to the Arctic Regions and migrates southward to Cuba. On Long Island it is a very common spring and fall migrant (*Dutcher*, MS.).

49. Lophodytes cucullatus (*Linn.*). HOODED MERGANSER. (131.)—North America generally, breeding locally throughout its range. Near New York it is a not common migrant and occasional winter visitant.

50. Anas bochas *Linn.* MALLARD. (132.)—Northern parts of the Northern Hemisphere. In America it is more common in the interior, and rarely breeds on the Atlantic coast south of Labrador. It is here an irregular transient visitant, occurring in spring, winter, and fall.

FIG. 4. MALLARDS.

*51. **Anas obscura** *Gmel.* BLACK DUCK. (133.)—Breeds from New Jersey to Labrador and winters from Massachusetts southward. It formerly nested in this vicinity, but now is found chiefly as a migrant, and less commonly in the winter. It still nests at some points on the Jersey coast, and in a few localities on Long Island (*Dutcher*, MS.). (See Group, main floor, opposite Case F.)

52. **Anas strepera** *Linn.* GADWALL. (135.)—Northern Hemisphere; in America more common in the interior, breeding locally from Kansas northward. It is found only as a very rare migrant in this vicinity.

53. **Anas penelope** *Linn.* EUROPEAN WIDGEON. (136.)—An Old World species which occurs rarely on our coasts. It has been taken at Leonia, New Jersey (*Chapman*, Auk, VI, 1889, p. 302).

54. **Anas americana** *Gmel.* BALDPATE; AMERICAN WIDGEON. (137.)—Breeds in the interior, from Minnesota northward; not common on the Atlantic coast except from Virginia southward in winter. In this vicinity it is an irregular transient visitant.

55. **Anas crecca** *Linn.* EUROPEAN GREEN-WINGED TEAL. (138.)—An Old World species of rare occurrence on our coasts. It is recorded from Trenton, N. J. (*Abbott*, Geology of New Jersey, 1868, p. 792), and Hartford, Conn. (*Treat*, Auk, VIII, 1891, p. 112).

PLATE II. BLACK DUCK.
(From Group in American Museum of Natural History.)

56. Anas carolinensis *Gmel.* GREEN-WINGED TEAL. (139.)
—Breeds from Minnesota and New Brunswick northward, and winters thence southward to the West Indies. With us it is a rather uncommon spring and fall migrant and winter resident.

57. Anas discors *Linn.* BLUE-WINGED TEAL. (140.)—Breeds from the northern Mississippi Valley and New Brunswick northward and winters from Virginia to northern South America. It is here a rare spring and common fall migrant.

58. Spatula clypeata (*Linn.*). SHOVELLER; SPOONBILL. (142)—Northern Hemisphere; in North America, breeding locally in the interior, from Texas northward. In this vicinity the Shoveller is a rare and irregular transient visitant.

59. Dafila acuta (*Linn.*). PINTAIL; SPRIGTAIL. (143.)—Northern Hemisphere; in North America breeds in the interior from Iowa and Illinois northward; winters from the Middle States southward to the West Indies. Near New York it is a common migrant.

*****60. Aix sponsa** (*Linn.*). WOOD DUCK; SUMMER DUCK. (144.) —"Temperate North America, breeding throughout its range." The Wood Duck is a rare summer resident on some of our more retired, wooded streams, and becomes more common during the migrations.

61. Netta rufina (*Pall.*). RUFOUS-CRESTED DUCK. (145.)—This is an Old World species which is known as North American only from one specimen found in Fulton Market, New York City, and supposed to have been shot on Long Island.

62. Aythya americana (*Eyt.*). REDHEAD. (146.)—North America, breeding from California and Maine northward, and wintering from Virginia southward. On Long Island this species occurs as a regular migrant, in varying numbers, and is occasionally found in the winter (*Dutcher*, MS.).

FIG. 5. REDHEAD.

63 Aythya vallisneria (*Wils.*). CANVAS-BACK. (147.)—North America, breeding only in the interior, from Minnesota northward, and wintering from the Chesapeake southward. It occurs here as a rare migrant.

FIG. 6. CANVAS-BACK.

64. Aythya marila nearctica *Stejn.* AMERICAN SCAUP DUCK; BROAD-BILL; BLUE-BILL; BLACK-HEAD; RAFT DUCK. (148.)— North America, breeding in the interior from Manitoba northward. It is the commonest Duck of our bays where it is sometimes seen in great numbers. It appears from the north about October 1, and remains until its feeding grounds are frozen over, returning as soon as the ice breaks in the early spring.

65 Aythya affinis (*Eyt.*). LESSER SCAUP DUCK; LITTLE BLUE-BILL; CREEK BROAD-BILL; RAFT DUCK. (149.)—Not so common as the preceding, with which its range in the main agrees.

66. Aythya collaris (*Donov.*). RING-NECKED DUCK. (150.) —North America, breeding only in the interior, from Iowa northward. It is here a very rare irregular transient visitant.

67. Glaucionetta clangula americana (*Bonap.*). AMERICAN GOLDEN-EYE; WHISTLER. (151.)—North America; breeding from Manitoba and Maine northward, and wintering from the southern limit of its breeding range to the West Indies. In favorable localities within our limits the Whistler is a not uncommon migrant and winter resident.

68 Charitonetta albeola (*Linn*). BUFFLE-HEAD; BUTTER-BALL. (153.)—Breeds from Iowa and Maine northward, and winters from near the southern limit of its breeding range to the West Indies. It is a not uncommon migrant and winter resident in this vicinity.

69. Clangula hyemalis (*Linn.*). OLD-SQUAW; OLD-WIFE; SOUTH-SOUTHERLY. (154.)—Breeds in the far north and winters southward to Virginia. With us it is a common winter resident.

70. Histrionicus histrionicus (*Linn.*). HARLEQUIN DUCK. (155.)—Breeds from Newfoundland northward, and winters southward to New Jersey. A very rare winter visitant off our coast. (See *Dutcher*, Auk, III, 1886, p. 434; VI, 1889, p. 134.)

Camptolaimus labradorius (*Gmel.*). LABRADOR DUCK. (156.)—"Formerly Northern Atlantic coast, from New Jersey (in winter) northward, breeding from Labrador northward." Doubtless now extinct. The Labrador Duck was apparently once a not uncommon winter bird on Long Island. In a paper by Mr. William Dutcher (Auk, VIII, 1891, p. 201), summarizing our knowledge of its life-history and enumerating the extant specimens, Mr. George

N. Lawrence is quoted as saying: "I recollect that about forty or more years ago it was not unusual to see them in Fulton Market, and without doubt they were killed on Long Island; at one time I remember seeing six fine males, which hung in the market until spoiled for want of a purchaser." Only forty-two of these Ducks have been recorded as existing in collections. Of this number seven are in the American Museum. (See Group, main floor, opp. Case E.)

71. **Somateria dresseri** *Sharpe.* AMERICAN EIDER. (160.) —Breeds from the Bay of Fundy to Labrador and winters southward to the Delaware. It his here a rare winter visitant.

72. **Somateria spectabilis** (*Linn.*). KING EIDER. (162.)— Breeds from Labrador to the Arctic Regions, migrating southward regularly as far as eastern Long Island (*Dutcher*, Auk, V, 1888, p. 175).

73. **Oidemia americana** *Sw. & Rich.* AMERICAN SCOTER; BLACK COOT (163.)—Breeds from Labrador northward, and in winter is found as far south as Virginia. In our waters it is a more or less common migrant and winter resident.

74. **Oidemia deglandi** *Bonap.* WHITE-WINGED SCOTER; WHITE-WINGED COOT. (165.)—Breeds from Labrador northward, and winters southward to Virginia. It is a common migrant and winter visitant off our coasts.

75. **Oidemia perspicillata** (*Linn.*). SURF SCOTER. (166.)— Breeds from the Gulf of St. Lawrence northward, and winters southward to Virginia. It is found here with the preceding species.

76. **Erismatura rubida** (*Wils.*). RUDDY DUCK. (167.)— Found from northern South America to the Fur Countries, breeding locally throughout its range. With us it is a not uncommon migrant, occurring in varying numbers.

77. **Chen hyperborea nivalis** (*Forst.*). GREATER SNOW GOOSE. (169*a*.)—Breeds in the far north and migrates southward, casually to Cuba. In this vicinity it is an irregular transient visitant.

78. **Chen cærulescens** (*Linn.*). BLUE GOOSE. (169.1.)— Breeds in the Hudson's Bay region, and migrates chiefly through the interior to Texas. It is a rare bird on the Atlantic coast. The only record for this vicinity is based on a specimen killed on Shinnecock Bay, L I. (*Dutcher*, Auk, X, 1893, p. 270).

79. Anser albifrons gambeli (*Hartl.*). AMERICAN WHITE-FRONTED GOOSE. (171*a*.)—North America, breeding far northward; in winter, south to Mexico and Cuba. Rare on the Atlantic coast. It has been recorded on Long Island from Babylon (*Giraud*), Great South Bay, Islip, and Montauk (*Dutcher*, Auk, X, 1893, p. 271).

*80. Branta canadensis (*Linn*.). CANADA GOOSE. (172.)—Breeds from Newfoundland and Minnesota northward, and migrates southward to the West Indies and Mexico. It is here a common migrant, appearing in November and remaining until our bays are frozen. In the spring the last birds pass on their northward journey as late as early May.

FIG. 7. CANADA GOOSE.

81. Branta canadensis hutchinsii (*Sw. & Rich.*). HUTCHINS'S GOOSE. (172*a*.)—Breeds within the Arctic Circle and migrates southward, chiefly through the Mississippi Valley. It is a rare migrant in this vicinity.

82. Branta bernicla (*Linn.*). BRANT. (173.)—Breeds within the Arctic Circle; in North America, migrates southward along the Atlantic coast, reaching North Carolina in winter. It is here a common bird, appearing from the north in October and remaining until our bays are frozen, when it retreats farther southward. In April it returns and the migration is not concluded until May.

83. Branta nigricans (*Lawr.*). BLACK BRANT. (174.)—This is a western species which is occasionally found on our coasts It has been recorded from Egg Harbor, N. J. (*Lawrence*), Babylon and Islip, L. I. (*Dutcher*, Auk, 1893, pp. 266, 271).

84. Branta leucopsis (*Bechst.*). BARNACLE GOOSE. (175.)—An Old World species, occurring accidentally on our coasts. A specimen was killed on Jamaica Bay, L. I., in October, 1876 (*Lawrence*, Bull. Nutt. Orn. Club, II, 1877, p. 18).

85. Olor columbianus (*Ord.*). WHISTLING SWAN. (180.)—Breeds in the far north, and winters as far south as the Gulf of Mexico. It is an exceedingly rare bird on the Atlantic coast north of the Chesapeake.

Order HERODIONES. Herons, Storks, Ibises, etc.

Family IBIDIDÆ.—IBISES.

86. Guara alba (*Linn.*). WHITE IBIS. (184.)—A bird of the Southern States, which has been recorded twice from this vicinity, (Raynor South and Moriches, L. I., *Giraud*).

87. Plegadis autumnalis (*Hasselq.*). GLOSSY IBIS. (186.)—An Old World species of "irregular distribution in America." It has been recorded once from Southampton, L. I., and once from Carnarsie Bay, L. I. (*Dutcher*, Auk, X, 1893, p. 271).

Family ARDEIDÆ.—HERONS, EGRETS, BITTERNS, ETC.

*88. Botaurus lentiginosus (*Montag.*). AMERICAN BITTERN. (190.)—"Temperate North America, south to Guatemala and the West Indies"; breeds but rarely south of Virginia. In this vicinity it is not common during the summer.

89. Ardetta exilis (*Gmel.*). LEAST BITTERN. (191.)—Temperate and tropical America, breeding as far north as Maine. It is here a locally common summer resident.

90. **Ardea herodias** *Linn.* GREAT BLUE HERON. (194.)—
"North America, from the Arctic Regions southward to the West Indies and Northern South America." With us it is a common migrant, and in a few localities is found as a summer resident. It is generally known by the name of "Crane" or "Sandhill Crane."

91. **Ardea egretta** *Gmel.* AMERICAN EGRET (196.)—
A southern species, breeding as far north as Virginia, and after the breeding season wandering northward in small numbers. It is here a rare but apparently regular summer visitant, arriving about August 1, and remaining until the last of September (*Dutcher*, Auk, X, 1884, p. 32).

92. **Ardea candidissima** *Gmel.* SNOWY HERON. (197.)—
Has much the same range as the preceding species, and like it strays northward after the breeding season. It occurs in small numbers, but regularly, in some localities in this vicinity. One of three individuals seen near Sayville, L. I., May 30, 1885, by Messrs. William Dutcher and L. S. Foster was "carrying a long stick in its bill" (*Dutcher*, Auk, III, 1886, p. 435), and it is possible was preparing to breed.

93. **Ardea cærulea** *Linn.* LITTLE BLUE HERON. (200.)—
This southern species, like the preceding, wanders northward in small numbers after the breeding season, and a few are sometimes found near New York. (See Group, main floor, opposite Case D.)

*94. **Ardea virescens** *Linn.* GREEN HERON. (201.)—Breeds from the Bay of Fundy southward. It is one of our commonest Herons and is known under a great variety of names. It haunts the banks of streams and ponds, and places its nest of sticks in a bush or the lower branch of a tree.

*95. **Nycticorax nycticorax nævius** (*Bodd.*). BLACK-CROWNED NIGHT HERON; QUAWK. (202.)—Breeds from New Brunswick southward. It nests in colonies, placing a small platform-like nest in the upper branches of trees. There is a colony containing about 1000 pairs not far from New York City. The popular name "Quawk", is derived from the call of the bird.

96. **Nycticorax violaceus** (*Linn.*). YELLOW-CROWNED NIGHT HERON. 203.)—Breeds from South Carolina southward and occasionally strays up the coast as far as Massachusetts. There is but one definite record for this region, that of a specimen taken in April, near Freeport, Queens County, L. I. (*Dutcher*, Auk, X, 1893, p. 286).

Order PALUDICOLÆ. Cranes, Rails, etc.

Family RALLIDÆ.—RAILS, GALLINULES, AND COOTS.

97. Rallus elegans *Aud.* KING RAIL. (208.)—Breeds as far north as Connecticut, and has been known to stray to Maine. It is a rare summer resident of our fresh-water marshes (*Dutcher*, Auk, V, 1888, p. 176).

98. Rallus longirostris crepitans (*Gmel.*). CLAPPER RAIL; MEADOW HEN; MARSH HEN. (211.)—Salt-water marshes of eastern North America, breeding from Connecticut to the Gulf of Mexico. This is an exceedingly common summer resident, and is occasionally found in winter in the salt marshes of our coasts. The nest is placed on the ground among the meadow grasses. (See Group, main floor, between Cases O and P.)

99. Rallus virginianus *Linn.* VIRGINIA RAIL. (212.)—Breeds from Pennsylvania northward. In this vicinity it is a locally common summer resident, and a few remain during the winter.

100. Porzana carolina (*Linn.*). SORA; CAROLINA RAIL; RAIL-BIRD. (214.)—Breeds from Long Island northward, and winters from South Carolina to northern South America. It is a rather rare summer resident in this vicinity, but in the fall becomes common, feeding on the wild rice of our marshes where, however, it is yearly becoming less numerous.

101. Porzana noveboracensis (*Gmel.*). YELLOW RAIL. (215.)—"Eastern North America, from Nova Scotia and Hudson's Bay west to Utah and Nevada." Little is known about the nesting habits of this bird. It haunts grassy marshes and seeks safety by hiding or running, and for this reason is rarely seen. Several have been taken during the fall migration in this vicinity, and it is doubtless more common than is generally supposed.

102. Porzana jamaicensis (*Gmel.*). BLACK RAIL. (216.)—Temperate North America, north to Massachusetts, probably breeding throughout its range. This bird, though much rarer, has, as far as known, the same habits as the preceding species, and like it is very difficult to observe. It has been taken in the spring at Jamaica Bay, and doubtless breeds in this vicinity, as its nest has been found at Saybrook, Conn. (*Clark*, Auk, I, 1884, p. 394).

103. Crex crex (*Linn.*) CORN CRAKE. (217.)—This is an Old World species, which sometimes strays to Greenland and our Atlantic coast. In this vicinity there are records for Sag Harbor, L. I. (*Dutcher*, Auk, III, 1886, p. 435), Oakdale, L. I. (*ibid.*, Auk, V, 1888, p. 177), and Saybrook, Conn. (*Clark*, Orn. and Oöl., XIII, 1888, p. 45).

104. Ionornis martinica (*Linn.*). PURPLE GALLINULE. (218.) —Tropical America, breeding as far north as South Carolina, and straying casually to Maine. There are but two definite records for this region, — Middle Island, L. I. (*Helme*, Orn. and Oöl., VII, 1882, p. 118), and Indian Pond, near Flatlands, L. I. (*Dutcher*, Auk, X, 1893, p. 272).

105. Gallinula galeata (*Licht.*). FLORIDA GALLINULE. (219.) —Temperate and tropical America, breeding as far north as Maine, and wintering from Florida southward. It breeds only locally in the northeastern part of its range, frequenting the borders of ponds or streams surrounded by marshy grounds. Its nest has not been found in the immediate vicinity of New York City, where it is known only as a rare migrant.

*106. **Fulica americana** *Gmel.* COOT; MUD-HEN; CROW-DUCK (221.)—"North America, from Greenland and Alaska southward to the West Indies and Central America", breeding locally throughout its range. The Mud-hen is a not uncommon bird during the migration, but it is recorded as breeding only near Morristown, N. J. (*Thurber*, True Democratic Banner, newspaper, Nov. 10, 1887).

Order LIMICOLÆ. Shore Birds.

Family PHALAROPODIDÆ.—PHALAROPES.

107. Crymophilus fulicarius (*Linn.*). RED PHALAROPE. (222.)—Breeds in the Arctic regions, and migrates southward to the Middle States. The Phalaropes are pelagic birds, not often coming to our coasts unless driven shoreward by storms. There are both August and May records for this species on Long Island.

108. Phalaropus lobatus (*Linn.*). NORTHERN PALHAROPE. (223.)—"Northern portions of the Northern Hemisphere, breeding in Arctic latitudes; south in winter to the tropics." This bird occurs with us as a regular migrant, and after severe storms is sometimes common in flocks. (See *Dutcher*, Auk, 1884, p. 33.)

109. Phalaropus tricolor (*Vieill*). WILSON'S PHALAROPE. (224.)—Interior of North America, breeding from northern Illinois northward. With us it is a very rare and irregular migrant.

Family RECURVIROSTRIDÆ.—AVOCETS AND STILTS.

110. Recurvirostra americana (*Gmel.*). AMERICAN AVOCET. (225.)—A bird of the interior, breeding from Texas to the Saskatchewan. Giraud mentions it as casual on Long Island, and says that a few breed at Egg Harbor, N. J. Mr. William Dutcher records four individuals seen by Col. Nicolas Pike on Long Island as follows: Ponquogue, 1844; Carnarsie Bay, 1847; Southampton, two, no date (Auk, X, 1893, p. 272).

111. Himantopus mexicanus (*Müll.*). BLACK-NECKED STILT. (226.)—A southern species, breeding in the Gulf States and locally in the Mississippi Valley; rare on the Atlantic coast. Giraud mentions it as "unfrequent", and Mr. Dutcher records two specimens taken by Col. Pike on Great South Bay, one of them in 1843 (Auk, X, 1893, p. 272).

Family SCOLOPACIDÆ.—SNIPES, SANDPIPERS, ETC.

112. Scolopax rusticola *Linn.* EUROPEAN WOODCOCK. (227.) —The occurrence of this species in North America is of course accidental. The only record for this vicinity is based on a specimen found in Washington Market, December 6, 1859, which was said to have been killed near Shrewsbury, N. J. (*Lawrence*, Ann. Lyc. Nat. Hist., VIII, 1866, p. 223).

113. Philohela minor (*Gmel.*). WOODCOCK. (228.)—Eastern North America, north to Labrador and Manitoba, breeding throughout its range, and wintering from southern Illinois and Virginia southward. The Woodcock is a common summer resident in the vicinity of New York, and doubtless will remain so as long as it is protected by law during the summer. It arrives early in March, and does not leave us until the ground is frozen. (See Group, main floor, between Cases A and B.)

FIG. 8. WOODCOCK.

114. Gallinago delicata (*Ord*). WILSON'S SNIPE; ENGLISH SNIPE. (230.)--North America, breeding from Connecticut and northern Illinois northward to Labrador, and wintering from southern Illinois and South Carolina to northern South America. In this vicinity it is a not uncommon migrant, and crippled birds are said to have nested on several occasions near Chatham, N. J. (*Herrick*, Forest and Stream, XII, 1879, p. 165). During mild seasons a few pass the winter here (*Dutcher*, MS.).

115. Macrorhamphus griseus (*Gmel.*) DOWITCHER (231.) --North America, breeding in the Arctic Regions, and wintering from Florida southward. With us it is a common migrant, arriving from the south about May 1, and returning from the north between July 10 and August 15.

Migrating Snipe, Sandpipers, and Plovers fly, as a rule, some distance off the land and if the weather is calm and clear, very few birds occur on our shores. If, however, during their migrations storms from the right quarter, or fogs occur, many birds are driven shoreward and there results what among sportsmen is known as a 'flight'.

116. Macrorhamphus scolopaceus (*Say*). LONG-BILLED DOWITCHER. (232.)--Western North America, breeding in Alaska.

This western representative of our common Dowitcher is a rare but regular late fall migrant along the Atlantic coast.

117. Micropalama himantopus (*Bonap.*). STILT SAND-PIPER. (233.)—Breeds within the Arctic Circle and migrates southward in winter to South America. It is here a not common but by no means rare migrant, occurring chiefly during the fall migration from the middle of July to the middle of September.

118. Tringa canutus *Linn.* KNOT; ROBIN SNIPE. (234.)—Breeds within the Arctic Circle and winters from Florida southward. In this vicinity it is a common migrant, passing northward during May, and returning from the middle of July to the first of October.

119. Tringa maritima *Brünn.* PURPLE SANDPIPER. (235.)—Breeds within the Arctic Circle, and migrates southward, reaching Long Island, where it is a rare but regular winter resident.

120. Tringa maculata *Vieill.* PECTORAL SANDPIPER; KRIEKER. (239.)—Breeds in the Arctic Regions, and migrates in winter to South America. The Krieker, as it is locally known, is a common and sometimes abundant fall migrant in this vicinity but is less frequently seen in the spring. It returns from the north in early August, and its migration is concluded about the last of October.

121. Tringa fuscicollis *Vieill.* WHITE-RUMPED SANDPIPER. (240.)—Breeds in the Arctic Regions and migrates as far south as Patagonia. It is here a not uncommon spring and fall migrant.

122. Tringa bairdii (*Coues*). BAIRD'S SANDPIPER. (241.)—This is a bird of the interior of North America, breeding within the Arctic Regions and migrating southward to South America. It is rare or casual on the Atlantic coast. There are several records for this vicinity as follows: Rockaway, L. I., August, two specimens, and September, two specimens (*N. T. Lawrence*, Forest and Stream, X, 1878, p. 235), and Far Rockaway, L. I., August, one specimen (*N. T. Lawrence*, Auk, II, 1885, p. 273).

123. Tringa minutilla *Vieill.* LEAST SANDPIPER; PEEP; MEADOW OXEYE. (242.)—Breeds in the Arctic Regions and winters from the Gulf States to Patagonia. This is one of our commonest Sandpipers, and with the Semipalmated Sandpiper, is the little "Peep" or "Oxeye" seen in small flocks running along our shores and beaches. It passes northward during May and returns about July 10, the fall migration being concluded about September 1.

124. Tringa alpina pacifica (*Coues*). RED-BACKED SANDPIPER; LEAD-BACK. (243a.)—Breeds in the Arctic Regions and winters from Florida southward. This is a very common migrant on our coasts, but is less common in the spring than in the fall. It migrates northward in early May and returns about September 1, remaining until November.

The Dunlin (*Tringa alpina*), the European representative of the preceding, from which it differs only slightly, has been taken once at Shinnecock Bay, L. I. (*Young*, Auk, X, 1893, p. 78).

125. Tringa ferruginea *Brünn*. CURLEW SANDPIPER. (244.) —"Old World in general, occasional in eastern North America." There are several records of its occurrence on Long Island.

126. Ereunetes pusillus (*Linn.*). SEMIPALMATED SANDPIPER; PEEP; SAND-OXEYE. (246.)—Breeds in the Arctic Regions, and winters from Florida to South America. This is our most common Sandpiper, and during its fall migration is abundant along our shores in small flocks. It migrates northward during May, returns about July 10, and the fall migration is not concluded until about October 1.

127. Ereunetes occidentalis *Lawr*. WESTERN SANDPIPER. (247.)—This is the western representative of the preceding. It is not infrequently found on our coast, generally associated with *E. pusillus*.

128. Calidris arenaria (*Linn.*). SANDERLING; SURF SNIPE. (248.)—Breeds in the Arctic Regions, and in America migrates as far south as Patagonia. It is an abundant migrant along our coasts, where, as a rule, it is found on the outer beaches. It passes northward during May, and returns on its southward journey about July 10, from which date until October it is more or less numerous.

129. Limosa fedoa (*Linn.*). MARBLED GODWIT; BROWN MARLIN. (249.)—Breeds chiefly in the interior, from Minnesota northward, and winters as far south as Central America and Cuba. This is a rare bird on the Atlantic coast, where it occurs only as an irregular fall visitant.

130. Limosa hæmastica (*Linn.*). HUDSONIAN GODWIT; RING-TAILED MARLIN. (251.)—Eastern North America, breeding in the Arctic Regions and migrating as far south as Patagonia

In this vicinity the Ring-tail Marlin is an irregular fall migrant (*Dutcher*, Auk, III, 1889, p. 437).

*131. Totanus melanoleucus (*Gmel.*). GREATER YELLOW-LEGS. (254.)—Breeds from Labrador northward, and winters from the Gulf States to Patagonia. It is a common migrant, arriving in the spring about the latter half of April, and returning in the latter half of July, the migration not being concluded until November.

132. Totanus flavipes (*Gmel.*). YELLOW-LEGS; SUMMER YELLOW-LEGS. (255.)—Breeds chiefly in the interior, from the Northern States northward, and winters from the Gulf States to Patagonia. With us it is very rare in the spring but is abundant during its southward migration, which begins about July 15 and ends in September.

133. Totanus solitarius (*Wils.*). SOLITARY SANDPIPER. (256.)—Breeds from the Northern States northward, and winters in South America. It passes northward in May and returns in July. It is not a true shore-bird, but is more frequently found near fresh-water ponds and streams.

134. Symphemia semipalmata (*Gmel.*). WILLET. (258.)—Eastern North America, breeding regularly from Florida to southern New Jersey, and locally and rarely as far as Nova Scotia. In this vicinity it occurs only as a fall migrant. It is probable that the Western Willet (*S. s. inornata*) is also occasionally found on our coasts.

135. Pavoncella pugnax (*Linn.*). RUFF. (260.)—"Northern parts of the Old World, straying occasionally to eastern North America." There are three specimens of this bird in the American Museum from North America, two of which, in the Lawrence Collection, are labeled "Long Island", while the third is in the Elliot Collection and is labeled "Barnegat, N. J."

136. Bartramia longicauda (*Bechst.*). BARTRAMIAN SANDPIPER; UPLAND PLOVER; FIELD PLOVER. (261.)—Breeds from Virginia and Kansas to Nova Scotia aud Alaska, and winters in South America. In the vicinity of New York City it is found as a rather rare migrant and still rarer summer resident. It arrives about the middle of April and frequents fields and pastures.

137. Tryngites subruficollis (*Vieill.*). BUFF-BREASTED SANDPIPER. (262.)—A bird of the interior, breeding in the far north and wintering in South America. It is very rare on the Atlantic coast. Giraud records "a party of five" as seen in August on Gowanus Bay; four specimens have been taken at Rockaway in August and September (*N. T. Lawrence*, Forest and Stream, X, 1879, p. 235); one was taken in August at Montauk Point (*Berier*, Bull. N. O. C., VI, 1880, p 126); and Mr. Dutcher mentions an August specimen from Suffolk County and a midsummer bird from Shinnecock Bay (Auk, VI, 1889, p. 136).

*****138. Actitis macularia** (*Linn.*). SPOTTED SANDPIPER; TIP-UP. (263.)—South America, and North America to Labrador, breeding throughout its North American range. This is the common summer Sandpiper so frequently seen on our ponds, streams, and beaches.

139. Numenius longirostris *Wils.* LONG-BILLED CURLEW; SICKLE-BILL. (264.)—Breeds in the interior as far north as Manitoba, and on the Atlantic coast as far as North Carolina. It is here a rare and irregular fall visitant.

140. Numenius hudsonicus *Lath.* HUDSONIAN CURLEW; JACK CURLEW. (265.)—Breeds in the Arctic Regions, and winters from the Gulf States to Patagonia. The "Jack Curlew", as it is locally known, is a not uncommon migrant in this vicinity. It passes northward in May, and the southern migration occurs between the middle of July and the first of October.

141. Numenius borealis (*Forst.*). ESKIMO CURLEW; DOUGH-BIRD; FUTE. (266.)—Breeds in the Arctic Regions and winters in South America. Mr. Dutcher is of the opinion that this bird migrates some distance off the coasts; it is found on our shores only after heavy storms.

Family CHARADRIIDÆ.—PLOVERS.

142. Vanellus vanellus (*Linn.*). LAPWING. (269.)—An Old World species, of accidental occurrence in America. The only record for Eastern North America south of Greenland is that of a specimen shot at Merrick, L. I., December, 1883 (*Dutcher*, Auk, III, 1886, p. 438).

143. Charadrius squatarola (*Linn.*). BLACK-BELLIED PLOVER; BEETLE-HEAD. (270.)—Breeds in the Arctic Regions and in

America winters as far south as Brazil. With us it is a common migrant, more numerous in the fall. It passes northward from about April 15 to June 1, and the return migration occurs between August 1 and November 1.

144. Charadrius dominicus *Müll.* GOLDEN PLOVER; GREEN-BACK. (272.)—Breeds in the Arctic Regions, and winters from Florida to Patagonia. In this vicinity it is a rare spring and common fall migrant, occurring chiefly in September.

*145. Ægialitis vocifera (*Linn.*). KILDEER. (273.)—Breeds from Florida to Manitoba, and winters from Virginia to South America. In the neighborhood of New York City the Kildeer is a rare summer resident and not uncommon migrant. It arrives in March and remains with us until November.

146. Ægialitis semipalmata *Bonap.* SEMIPALMATED PLOVER; RING-NECK. (274.)—Breeds from Labrador northward, and winters from the Gulf States to Brazil. The Ring-neck is one of our commonest shore-birds. It passes northward in May and returns about July 15, the fall migration not being concluded until October 1.

147. Ægialitis meloda (*Ord*). PIPING PLOVER. (277.)—Eastern North America, breeding from Virginia to Newfoundland, and wintering from Florida southward. It is here a rare summer resident, arriving in April and remaining until September.

148. Ægialitis meloda circumcincta *Ridgw.* BELTED PIPING PLOVER. (277*a*.)—This is a representative of the preceding, which sometimes occurs on our coasts. There is but one record for this vicinity. (Rockaway, L. I., April 30, 1873, adult male, *Eagle*, Bull. N. O. C., III, 1878, p. 94.)

149. Ægialitis wilsonia (*Ord*). WILSON'S PLOVER. (280.)—Breeds as far north as Virginia, and strays casually to Nova Scotia. There are several records for Long Island (*Dutcher*, Bull. N. O. C., IV, 1879, p. 242; Auk, III, 1886, p. 438 — Shinnecock Bay), and one for Bridgeport, Conn. (*Averill*, List of Birds found in the Vicinity of Bridgeport, 1892, p. 9).

Family APHRIZIDÆ. —SURF BIRDS AND TURNSTONES.

150. Arenaria interpres (*Linn.*). TURNSTONE; BRANT BIRD; CALICO-BACK. (283.)—Breeds in the Arctic Regions, and migrates as far south as Patagonia. With us it is a common migrant, passing northward in May, returning about August 1, and remaining until September.

Family HÆMATOPODIDÆ.—OYSTER-CATCHERS.

151. Hæmatopus palliatus *Temm.* OYSTER-CATCHER. (286.) —Breeds as far north as southern New Jersey and occasionally strays to Nova Scotia. It is here of rare and irregular occurrence (*Dutcher*, Auk, X, 1893, p. 272).

Order GALLINÆ. Gallinaceous Birds.

Family TETRAONIDÆ.—GROUSE, PARTRIDGES, ETC.

*152. Colinus virginianus (*Linn.*). BOB-WHITE; QUAIL. (289.)—Eastern North America, from southern Maine and Minnesota southward to the Gulf of Mexico; resident wherever found. Quail are not uncommon in the vicinity of New York, but they are so eagerly hunted that, as the country becomes more thickly settled, only the most rigid enforcement of the game-laws will preserve them from extermination.

*153. Bonasa umbellus (*Linn.*). RUFFED GROUSE; PARTRIDGE. (300.)—Eastern United States, from Vermont to Virginia, and along the Alleghanies to northern Georgia. Partridges are much less common with us than Quails. They are birds of the woods, and for this reason disappear with the forests, while Quails, on the contrary, become more numerous as the country is cleared. (See Group, main floor, opposite Case I.)

In the early part of this century Pinnated Grouse or Prairie Hens (*Tympanuchus cupido*) were abundant in some parts of Long Island, but they have been extinct for about sixty years (*Giraud*, Birds of Long Island, p. 195, and *Dutcher*, Auk, X, 1893, p. 272).

Order COLUMBÆ. Pigeons.

Family COLUMBIDÆ.—DOVES AND PIGEONS.

154. Ectopistes migratorius (*Linn.*). PASSENGER PIGEON; WILD PIGEON. (315.)—Eastern North America, northward in the interior to Hudsons Bay, breeding locally throughout the more northern part of its range. Fifty years ago the Wild Pigeon was an abundant bird in the vicinity of New York, but here, as elsewhere throughout its range, it has become very rare. In place of the thousands that used to visit us it is now observed irregularly and rarely. (*Lawrence*, Auk, VI, 1889, p. 196, and *Dutcher*, Auk, X, 1893, p. 274.)

*155. **Zenaidura macroura** (*Linn.*). MOURNING DOVE. (316.) —Breeds throughout temperate North America, from southern Canada to the Gulf. It is here a common summer resident, and under favorable circumstances passes the winter.

156. **Columbigallina passerina terrestris** *Chapm.* GROUND DOVE. (320.)—This is a species of the South Atlantic and Gulf States. It has been once taken in this vicinity (*Grinnell*, Bull. N. O. C., III, 1878, p. 147), but its occurrence is purely accidental and it is possible the specimen captured may have been an escaped cage-bird.

Order RAPTORES. Birds of Prey.

Family CATHARTIDÆ.—AMERICAN VULTURES.

157. **Cathartes aura** (*Linn.*) TURKEY VULTURE; TURKEY BUZZARD. (325.)—Temperate North America, from New Jersey southward to Patagonia. Of more or less regular occurrence in New Jersey as far north as Princeton in the interior and Sandy Hook on the coast. It is also occasionally seen on Long Island. A recent record notes the occurrence of a flock of eight birds of this species in Orange County, N. Y. (*Reynolds*, Forest and Stream, XVIII, 1894, p. 181).

158. **Catharista atrata** (*Bartr.*). BLACK VULTURE. (326.) —Breeds from North Carolina southward, and occasionally strays as far north as Maine. There are records for Sandy Hook, N J. (*Robt. B. Lawrence*, Bull. N. O. C., V, 1880, p. 116), and Coney Island, L. I. (*Berier*, Bull. N. O. C., VI, 1881, p. 126).

Family FALCONIDÆ.—FALCONS, HAWKS, EAGLES, ETC.

159. **Elanoides forficatus** (*Linn.*). SWALLOW-TAILED KITE. (327.)—Southern United States north to Pennsylvania and casually to Massachusetts, south to South America. In this vicinity it has been recorded from Raynor South, L.I. (*Giraud*, Birds of Long

Island, p. 13), "South shore of Long Island" (*Berier*, Bull. N. O. C., VI, 1881, p 126), and Chatham, N. J. (*Herrick*, Forest and Stream, XII, 1879, p. 165).

160. Circus hudsonius (*Linn.*). MARSH HAWK. (331.)—
—North America in general, south to Panama. This species remains with us throughout the year and is one of our most common Hawks.

***161. Accipiter velox** (*Wils.*). SHARP-SHINNED HAWK. (332.)
—Breeds throughout the United States and winters from Connecticut to Central America. It is here a common summer and rare winter resident.

162. Accipiter cooperi (*Bonap.*). COOPER'S HAWK. (333.)—
Breeds from Newfoundland to the Gulf of Mexico, and winters from Pennsylvania to Mexico. With us it is a not uncommon summer, and rare winter resident. This bird, the Sharp-shinned, and the rare Duck Hawk and Goshawk, are the only species of our Hawks which habitually live on birds. The others feed largely on insects and small field-mice, and being thus actually beneficial should be protected by law.

163. Accipiter atricapillus (*Wils.*). GOSHAWK. (334.)—
Breeds from the northern United States northward and winters as far south as Virginia. It is here a rare winter visitant.

***164. Buteo borealis** (*Gmel.*). RED-TAILED HAWK (337.)—
Eastern North America, breeding throughout its range. The Red-tail is one of our commonest Hawks and is resident throughout the year.

165 Buteo lineatus (*Gmel.*). RED-SHOULDERED HAWK. (339.)
—Eastern North America, resident nearly throughout its range. It is probably our most common Hawk and with the Red-tail is the one to which the name Chicken, or Hen Hawk, is generally applied.

166. Buteo swainsoni *Bonap.* SWAINSON'S HAWK. (342.)
—A western species of rare occurrence on the Atlantic coast. There is apparently but one record of its capture near New York City, viz, that of a specimen shot near Cornwall, N. Y., October 14, 1892 (*Dutcher*, Auk, X, p. 83).

167. Buteo latissimus (*Wils.*). BROAD-WINGED HAWK. (343.)
—Breeds throughout eastern North America, from New Brunswick southward. With us it is a rather uncommon resident.

168. Archibuteo lagopus sancti-johannis (*Gmel.*). ROUGH-LEGGED HAWK. (347*a*.)—North America, breeding north of the United States and wintering as far south as Virginia. It is here a rather rare winter resident.

169. Aquila chrysaëtos (*Linn.*). GOLDEN EAGLE. (349.)—North America; of rare occurrence east of the Mississippi. It has been recorded from Islip, L. I. (*Giraud*), Carnarsie, L. I. (*Dutcher*), Gravesend, L. I. (*Johnson*), and Highland Falls, N. Y., where, Dr. Mearns states, it is occasionally observed and was formerly known to nest.

*****170. Haliætus leucocephalus** (*Linn.*). BALD EAGLE. (352.) —North America, breeding throughout its range. This Eagle is here a rather rare bird; it is said by Dr. Mearns to nest in the Highlands of the Hudson. On Long Island it is a not uncommon resident and breeds in several localities (*Dutcher*, MS.).

171. Falco islandus *Brünn.* WHITE GYRFALCON. (353.)—An arctic species, rarely visiting the United States. The only record for this vicinity is that of a specimen killed on Long Island in the winter of 1856 (*Lawrence*, Ann. Lyc. Nat. Hist., New York, VIII, 1866, p. 280).

172. Falco rusticolus obsoletus (*Gmel.*). BLACK GYRFALCON. (354*b*.)—"Labrador, south in winter to Maine and New York." There is but one record of its occurrence in this vicinity, viz., a specimen shot in the fall of 1875, near Flushing, L. I. (*Berier*, Bull. N. O. C, VI, 1881, pp. 126, 247). I have not seen the specimens upon which these records are based. Our Gyrfalcons are difficult birds to identify and it is quite possible that the species here recorded may have been wrongly named.

173. Falco peregrinus anatum (*Bonap.*). DUCK HAWK. (356.)—North America and the greater part of South America, breeding from our Southern States northward. This Falcon, the "noble Peregrine" of Falconry, is a not uncommon migrant, especially along our coast, and is a rare summer resident along the Palisades and Highlands of the Hudson, where it is known to breed.

174. Falco columbarius *Linn.* PIGEON HAWK. (257.)—Breeds from the northern United States northward, and winters from the Southern States southward. It is here a common migrant, occurring chiefly an our coasts.

*175. **Falco sparverius** *Linn.* AMERICAN SPARROW HAWK. (360.)—Breeds from Florida to Hudson Bay, and winters from New Jersey southward. With us it is a not common resident but abundant migrant on our coasts (*Dutcher*, MS.)

*176. **Pandion haliaëtus carolinensis** (*Gmel.*). AMERICAN OSPREY; FISH HAWK. (364.)—Breeds from Florida to Labrador, and winters from South Carolina to northern South America. At certain localities along our coasts the Fish Hawk is found nesting in colonies.

FIG. 9. AMERICAN OSPREY.

Family STRIGIDÆ.—BARN OWLS.

177. **Strix pratincola** *Bonap.* AMERICAN BARN OWL. (365.) —Occasionally found as far north as Massachusetts, and breeds from Long Island southward through Mexico. The Barn Owl is here a rare but regular summer resident.

Family BUBONIDÆ.—HORNED OWLS, ETC.

178. Asio wilsonianus (*Less.*). AMERICAN LONG-EARED OWL. (366.)—Breeds from Nova Scotia and Manitoba southward to the Gulf States It is here a rather uncommon resident.

179. Asio accipitrinus (*Pall.*). SHORT-EARED OWL. (367.) —Nearly cosmopolitan, breeding in the United States from Virginia northward. With us it is common during the migrations, and while a few probably breed, there is no definite record of their doing so.

FIG. 10. SHORT-EARED OWL.

*180. Syrnium nebulosum (*Forst.*). BARRED OWL. (368.)— Eastern North America, northward to Nova Scotia and Manitoba; resident, except at the northern limit of its range. Next to the Screech Owl this is our commonest Owl. Its loud, sonorous hooting, *whoo, whoo, whoo, too-whoo, too whoo-ah*, is most frequently heard in the spring, and is familiar to many who are not acquainted with its author.

181. Scotiaptex cinerea (*Gmel.*). GREAT GRAY OWL. (370.)
—Breeds from Hudson Bay northward, and wanders southward in winter to the northern border of the United States. An individual shot near Mendham, N. J., is the only one which has been recorded from near New York City. (*Thurber*, True Democratic Banner, newspaper, Morristown, N. J., Nov. 10, 1887.)

***182. Nyctala acadica** (*Gmel*). SAW-WHET OWL, (372.)—Breeds from northern New York northward, and migrates southward in winter as far as Virginia. With us a regular, and, in some localities, a not uncommon winter resident.

***183. Megascops asio** (*Linn.*). SCREECH OWL. (373.)—Eastern North America, northward to New Brunswick and Minnesota; generally resident throughout its range. The Screech Owl is the commonest and best known of our Owls. (See Group, main floor, between Cases L and M.)

184. Bubo virginianus (*Gmel.*). GREAT HORNED OWL. (375.)—Eastern North America, northward to Labrador and southward to Costa Rica; resident throughout its range. With us a rather rare resident. This is the only one of our Owls which habitually preys upon poultry; the others feed almost exclusively on small field-mice and shrews.

***185. Nyctea nyctea** (*Linn.*). SNOWY OWL. (376.)—Breeds from Labrador northward and wanders southward in winter regularly to the northern United States and occasionally to Texas. It is here an irregular winter visitant, sometimes occurring in considerable numbers.

186. Surnia ulula caparoch (*Müll.*). HAWK OWL. (377*a*.)
—Breeds from Newfoundland northward, and occasionally wanders southward in winter as far as Pennsylvania. There is apparently but one record of its capture in this vicinity, — that of a specimen shot near Bay Ridge, L. I. (*Dutcher*, Auk, X, 1893, p. 275).

Order COCCYGES. Cuckoos, etc.

Family CUCULIDÆ.—CUCKOOS, ANIS, ETC.

*187. **Coccyzus americanus** (*Linn.*). YELLOW-BILLED CUCKOO. (387.)—Breeds from Florida to New Brunswick and winters in Central and South America. It is here a common summer resident, arriving about May 10, and departing the last of September. (See Group, Gallery, between Cases B and C.)

*188. **Coccyzus erythrophthalmus** (*Wils.*). BLACK-BILLED CUCKOO. (380.)—Breeds as far north as Labrador, and winters in Central and South America. With us it is a common summer resident arriving and departing at about the same time as the preceding species.

Family ALCEDINIDÆ.—KINGFISHERS.

*189. **Ceryle alcyon** (*Linn.*). BELTED KINGFISHER. (390.)—Breeds from Florida to Labrador, and winters from Virginia to South America. It is here a common summer resident, arriving the latter part of March and remaining until the streams and ponds, from which it obtains its food, are frozen.

Order PICI. Woodpeckers.

Family PICIDÆ.—WOODPECKERS.

*190. **Dryobates villosus** (*Linn.*). HAIRY WOODPECKER. (393.)—Eastern United States, from the northern border south to Virginia and the higher summits of North Carolina. In this vicinity it is a rather uncommon resident.

*191. **Dryobates pubescens** (*Linn.*). DOWNY WOODPECKER. (394.)—Eastern North America, from Labrador to Florida; resident throughout its range. It is one of our commonest Woodpeckers.

*192. **Dryobates borealis** (*Vieill.*). RED-COCKADED WOODPECKER. (395.)—Southern United States, westward to Indian Territory, and northward to Tennessee and Virginia. This bird is accidental near New York, the only record of its occurrence being based on a specimen taken at Hoboken, N. J. (*Lawrence*, Ann. Lyc. Nat. Hist., VIII, 1866, p. 291).

*193. **Sphyrapicus varius** (*Linn*). YELLOW-BELLIED WOODPECKER. (402.)—Breeds from Massachusetts northward, and winters from Virginia to Central America. It is here a common spring and fall migrant.

194. **Ceophlœus pileatus** (*Linn.*). PILEATED WOODPECKER. (405.)—"Formerly whole wooded region of North America; now rare or extirpated in the more thickly settled parts of the Eastern States." This large Woodpecker occurs near New York only as a rare straggler.

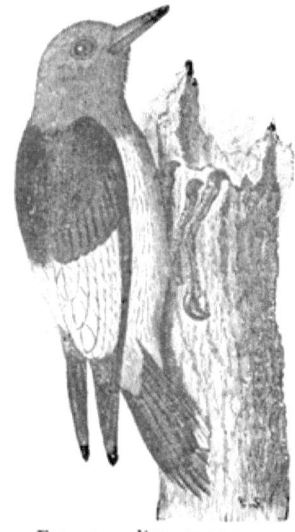

FIG. 11. RED-HEADED WOODPECKER.

*195. **Melanerpes erythrocephalus** (*Linn.*). RED-HEADED WOODPECKER. (406.)—Eastern North America, breeding from Florida to northern New York and Manitoba, and wintering from Virginia southward, and occasionally farther north. With us a summer resident of local distribution and a not uncommon, and sometimes abundant migrant.

196. **Melanerpes carolinus** (*Linn.*). RED-BELLIED WOODPECKER. (409.)—Eastern United States, breeding from Florida to Virginia and, in the interior, to Ontario and southern Dakota, occasionally strays to Massachusetts; winters from southern Ohio southward.

Giraud speaks of this bird as breeding on Long Island but it now occurs here only rarely and irregularly.

*197. **Colaptes auratus** (*Linn.*). FLICKER; HIGH-HOLE; CLAPE. (412.)—North America, west to the eastern slope of the Rocky Mountains and Alaska; breeds throughout its range, and winters from Illinois and southern New York southward. Our commonest Woodpecker. It is resident, but is much more common in the summer than in the winter.

Order MACROCHRIES. Goatsuckers, Swifts, etc.

Family CAPRIMULGIDÆ.—GOATSUCKERS.

*198. **Antrostomus vociferus** (*Wils.*). WHIP-POOR-WILL. (417.)—Eastern North America, north to New Brunswick and Manitoba; winters from Florida southward. In some localities near New York City the Whip-poor-will is a common summer resident. It arrives about May 1, and leaves about October 1.

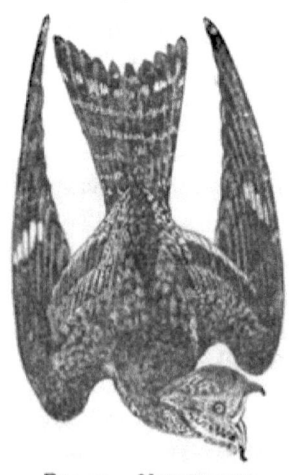

FIG. 12. NIGHTHAWK.

*199. **Chordeiles virginianus** (*Gmel.*). NIGHTHAWK. (420.)—Eastern North America, breeding from the Gulf States to Labrador, and wintering in South America. The Nighthawk is here a more or less common summer resident. Even in New York City, where it has been known to lay its eggs on the house-top, its characteristic note, *peent, peent*, uttered while it is coursing for food, is not infrequently heard. It arrives early in May and migrates southward in September and October, sometimes occurring at this season in large flocks.

*200. **Chætura pelagica** (*Linn.*). CHIMNEY SWIFT. (423.)—Eastern North America, breeding from Florida to Labrador, and wintering in Central America. With us it is an abundant summer resident, arriving the latter part of April and remaining until October. (See Group, main floor, opposite Case H.)

Family TROCHILIDÆ.—HUMMINGBIRDS.

*201. **Trochilus colubris** *Linn.* RUBY-THROATED HUMMINGBIRD. (428.)—Eastern North America, breeding from Florida to Labrabor, and wintering from southern Florida to Central America. This, the only species of Hummingbird found in eastern North America, is here a common summer resident, arriving early in May and remaining until October.

FIG. 13. RUBY-THROATED HUMMINGBIRDS AND NEST.

Order PASSERES. Perching Birds.

Family TYRANNIDÆ.—TYRANT FLYCATCHERS.

*202. **Tyrannus tyrannus** (*Linn.*). KINGBIRD. (444.)— North America north to New Brunswick and Manitoba, rare west of the Rocky Mountains: winters in Central and South America. The Kingbird is here a common summer resident, arriving early in May and remaining until October. (See Group, Gallery, between Cases K and L.)

203. **Tyrannus verticalis** *Say*. ARKANSAS KINGBIRD. (447.) —A western species; the only record for this vicinity is that of a young male taken at Riverdale, N. Y., October 19, 1875 (*Bicknell*, Bull. N. O. C., IV, 1879, p. 60).

*204. **Myiarchus crinitus** (*Linn.*). GREAT-CRESTED FLY-CATCHER. (432.)—Breeds from Florida to New Brunswick, and winters from southern Florida to Central America. With us a not uncommon summer resident, arriving early in May and remaining until September.

*205. **Sayornis phœbe** (*Lath.*). PHŒBE. (456.)—Eastern North America, breeding from South Carolina to Newfoundland and Manitoba, and wintering from North Carolina to Cuba and Mexico. In this vicinity it is a common summer resident, arriving about March 20, and leaving early in November.

206. **Contopus borealis** (*Swains.*). OLIVE-SIDED FLYCATCHER. (459.)—Breeds from Massachusetts and Minnesota northward, and winters in Central and South America. With us it occurs as a migrant, passing north in May, when it is apparently rare, and returning in the latter part of August when it is locally not uncommon.

*207. **Contopus virens** (*Linn.*). WOOD PEWEE. (461.)—Breeds from Florida to Newfoundland, and winters in Central America. It is a common summer resident of our woods, arriving about May 15 and remaining until the latter part of September.

*208. **Empidonax flaviventris** *Baird*. YELLOW-BELLIED FLYCATCHER. (463.)—Breeds from Berkshire County, Mass., to Labrador, and winters in Central America. It is here a rather rare spring, and not uncommon fall migrant, arriving in May and returning from its northern home early in August.

*209. **Empidonax acadicus** (*Gmel.*). ACADIAN FLYCATCHER. (465.)—Eastern United States, breeding from Florida to southern Connecticut and Manitoba, and wintering in Central America. A common summer resident of the Lower Hudson River Valley as far north as Sing Sing. On Long Island it apparently breeds only on the north shore, while there are but two records for Connecticut, — an adult taken at Suffield, June 24, 1874 (*Merriam*, Birds Conn., p. 58), and a nest with young at Greenwich, June 25, 1893 (*Voorhees*, Auk, XI, 1894, p. 259). (See Group, Gallery, between Cases I and J.)

210. **Empidonax pusillus traillii** (*Aud.*) TRAILL'S FLYCATCHER. (466a.)—Eastern North America, breeding from southern Illinois and Connecticut north to New Brunswick and Manitoba, and wintering in Central America. With us Traill's Flycatcher is a rather rare migrant and probably a rare summer resident. A nest and eggs, not fully identified, but with little doubt that of this species, was found by Mr. C. L. Brownell at Nyack.

*211. **Empidonax minimus** *Baird*. LEAST FLYCATCHER. (467.)—Eastern United States, breeding from Pennsylvania to

Quebec, and wintering in Central America. This species is a common summer resident in this vicinity; it arrives about May 1 and remains until late in September.

Family ALAUDIDÆ —LARKS.

Skylarks (*Alauda arvensis*) have from time to time been liberated near New York City. In 1887 a small colony had become established near Flatbush, L. I., where a nest containing young was found, but they have since disappeared (*Dutcher*, Auk, V, 1888, p. 180). At the present time the bird is not known to occur in this vicinity.

FIG. 14. HORNED LARK.

212. Otocoris alpestris (*Linn.*). HORNED LARK; SHORE LARK (474.)—Breeds in "Northern Europe, Greenland, Newfoundland, Labrador, and Hudson's Bay region; southward in winter into eastern United States to about Lat. 35°" (*Dwight*). This bird is a common winter resident. It is found at this season in most parts of Long Island but is infrequent in the Lower Hudson Valley.

213. Otocoris alpestris praticola *Hensh.* PRAIRIE HORNED LARK. (474*b*)—Breeds in the Upper Mississippi Valley eastward through New York to western Massachusetts and Long Island. This small race of the Horned Lark is of rather rare occurrence in this vicinity. It is apparently extending its range eastward and there is one record of its having probably bred on Long Island (*Dutcher*, Auk, V, 1888, p. 180), where it also occurs during the winter.

Family CORVIDÆ.—CROWS, JAYS, MAGPIES, ETC.

*214. **Cyanocitta cristata** (*Linn.*). BLUE JAY. (477.)—Eastern North America, breeding from Florida to Newfoundland; generally resident throughout its range. Here a common resident, more numerous during the fall migration than at other times of the year.

FIG. 15. BLUE JAY.

The Canada Jay (*Perisoreus canadensis*), a northern species which has only once been taken in Massachusetts (*Brewster*, Auk, VII, 1891, p. 91), is included by Mr. Lawrence in his "Catalogue of Birds" on the basis of an individual killed in July near Mahattanville, New York City. This specimen is now in the American Museum (No. 42,253). Its plumage is much worn and its toe-nails are abnormally long, facts which, taken in connection with the place and date of the bird's capture, induce me to believe that it had escaped from confinement.

215. Corvus corax principalis (*Wagl.*). AMERICAN RAVEN. (486a.)—United States, south to Guatemala; rare east of the Mississippi Now of very rare occurrence in this vicinity. It is said to have been formerly common on the northern New Jersey coast (*Lawrence*), and is still not uncommon along the southern coast of the State (*Stone*, Auk, XI, 1894, p. 137).

*216. Corvus americanus *Aud.* AMERICAN CROW. (488.)— "North America, from the Fur Countries to Mexico", wintering from the northern United States southward The Crow is here an abundant resident, but, as in the case of other species which are present the year around, it is probable that the individuals which summer with us pass the winter farther south, while our winter birds come to us from the north.

*217. Corvus ossifragus *Wils.* FISH CROW. (490.)—Gulf

and Atlantic coast, as far north as Long Island; resident throughout its range. A common inhabitant of the Lower Hudson River Valley as far north as Sing Sing and occasionally reaches Highland Falls. In Connecticut it is of regular occurrence as far east as Stratford (*Eames*, Auk, VI, 1889, p. 338), while on Long Island its exact status appears to be unknown, though it is probably not uncommon.

Family STURNIDÆ.—STARLINGS.

*****Sturnus vulgaris** *Linn.* STARLING. (493.)—This Old World species has been introduced into this country on several occasions, but only the last importation appears to have been successful. The birds included in this lot were imported, and released in Central Park, under the direction of Mr. Eugene Schiefflin of this city. They seem to have left the Park and to have established themselves in various places in the upper part of the city. A pair have bred for three successive seasons in the roof of this Museum. Mr. S. H. Chubb reports a pair nesting in a church at 122d st. and Lenox avenue, and they have also nested at 100th st. and Riverside Drive. Mr. C. B. Isham tells me he has found their nest at Kingsbridge, New York City, and that he repeatedly observed a flock of fifty birds in the same locality during the late summer and fall of 1893 and 1894.

Family ICTERIDÆ.—BLACKBIRDS, ORIOLES, ETC.

*****218. Dolichonyx oryzivorus** (*Linn.*). BOBOLINK; REED-BIRD. (494.)—Breeds from southern New Jersey northward to Nova Scotia, westward to Utah and northern Montana; leaves the United States by way of Florida and winters in South America. A locally distributed summer resident, arriving in early May and remaining until October. About the middle of July the males assume the Reed-bird plumage and resort to our wild-rice marshes, where they are joined by large numbers from the north, which pause to feed on the wild-rice.

Fifteen years ago the Bobolink was an abundant and generally distributed summer resident in this vicinity. Since that date it has rapidly decreased in numbers and is now entirely wanting in localities where it was formerly of regular occurrence.

Fig. 16. Bobolink.

*219. **Molothrus ater** (*Bodd.*). Cowbird. (495.)—Breeds from Texas to New Brunswick and Manitoba, and winters from southern Illinois southward. Here a common summer resident, arriving late in March and remaining until November. It has been recorded as occurring in winter (*Foster*, Abst. Proc. Linn. Soc., No. 5, 1893, p 2).

*220. **Agelaius phœniceus** (*Linn.*). Red-winged Blackbird. (498.)—Eastern North America, breeding from the Gulf of Mexico to New Brunswick and Manitoba, and wintering from Virginia southward. With us it is a common summer resident, abundant during the migrations when it occurs in large flocks. It is one of the first birds to reach us in the spring, frequently arriving before March 1, and it remains until December.

Fig. 17. Red-winged Blackbird.

*221. Sturnella magna (*Linn.*). MEADOW LARK. (501.)—
Eastern North America, breeding from the Gulf States to New Brunswick and Minnesota, and wintering from Massachusetts and Illinois southward. With us it is a common summer resident, occurring in reduced numbers during the winter, when it is largely confined to the extensive marshes near the coast.

*222. Icterus spurius (*Linn.*). ORCHARD ORIOLE. (506.)—
Eastern North America, breeding from the Gulf States to Massachusetts and Ontario; winters in Central America. In this vicinity it is a common summer resident, arriving early in May and remaining until September. (See Group, Gallery, between Cases F and G.)

*223. Icterus galbula (*Linn.*). BALTIMORE ORIOLE. (507.)—
Eastern North America, breeding from the Gulf States to New Brunswick, and wintering in Central America. It is here a somewhat more common summer resident than the preceding species. It arrives early in May and remains until September. (See Group, Gallery, between Cases D and E.)

*224. Scolecophagus carolinus (*Müll.*). RUSTY BLACKBIRD. (509.)—Breeds from New Brunswick and Manitoba northward to Labrador and Alaska; winters from Virginia southward. It is here a common migrant, passing northward in March, returning in September, and sometimes remaining until late in December.

*225. Quiscalus quiscula (*Linn.*). PURPLE GRACKLE; CROW BLACKBIRD. (511.)—Breeds in the Lower Mississippi Valley, and east of the Alleghanies from Georgia to Massachusetts; winters in the Southern States. It is here a common summer resident of local distribution, nesting in colonies. It is one of our earliest migrants, arriving from the south with the Red-winged Blackbird, about March 1. During the breeding season it is not seen far from the vicinity of its nest, but about July 1, when the young are on the wing, they gather in small flocks and wander over the country, pausing wherever they find an abundance of food. These flocks gradually coalesce, and in October and November form enormous gatherings numbering thousands of birds.

226. Quiscalus quiscula æneus (*Ridgw.*). BRONZED GRACKLE (511*b*.)—Breeds from Texas to Great Slave Lake, east to the Alleghanies, as far north as Pennsylvania, and north of this eastward to Connecticut and northward to Labrador, wintering largely in the Lower Mississippi Valley. With us it is apparently found only as a spring and fall migrant, sometimes not uncommon.

Family FRINGILLIDÆ.—FINCHES, SPARROWS, ETC.

227. Coccothraustes vespertina (*Coop.*). EVENING GROSBEAK. (514.)—Interior of North America, from Manitoba northward; southeastward in winter to the Upper Mississippi Valley and casually to the northern Atlantic States.

During the winter and early spring of 1890 there was a phenomenal incursion of Evening Grosbeaks into the northern United States. The most southern record of their occurrence in the Atlantic States was at Summit, N. J., where, on March 6, Mr. W. O. Raymond observed a flock of eight birds (Orn. and Oöl., XV, 1890, p. 46). No specimens were collected, but Mr. Raymond watched the birds for some time at a distance of about eight feet, and he has since examined skins of the species in this Museum, thus confirming his identification.

FIG. 18. PINE GROSBEAK.

228. Pinicola enucleator (*Linn.*). PINE GROSBEAK. (515.) —"Northern portions of the Northern Hemisphere, breeding far north; in winter south, in North America, irregularly to the northern United States." This species occurs here in the winter and then only at long and irregular intervals.

* **Passer domesticus** (*Linn.*). HOUSE SPARROW; ENGLISH SPARROW.—From the report of the Division of Economic Ornithology of the Department of Agriculture (Washington, 1889), we learn that English Sparrows were first introduced into New York City in 1860, when twelve birds were released in Madison Square. In 1864 they were introduced in Central Park, and in 1866 two hundred were set free in Union Park. From these, and one or two other small additional importations of a few pairs each, have descended the countless numbers of Sparrows which to-day inhabit our streets and parks. In this latitude the English Sparrow has been known to rear six broods in a season, and their marvellous rate of increase is graphically given in a table in the Report already mentioned, which shows that in ten years the progeny of a single pair might amount to 275, 716, 983, 698!

With the discordant notes of these ubiquitous little pests constantly in our ears we may read with mixed humor and regret the following quotation from Mr. Lawrence's Catalogue of New York Birds (Ann. Lyc. Nat. Hist., VIII, 1866, p. 287): "I first observed them in the spring of 1865. A friend, conversant with our local native birds, informed me that he had seen a species in the shrubbery around the church on the corner of 5th avenue and 29th street, with which he was not familiar; on going to ascertain what they were, to my surprise I found them to be House Sparrows; they were domiciled in the ivy which grew on the walls of the church, and were quite gentle and fearless, some alighting in the street and dusting themselves quite near to where I stood."

The European Chaffinch (*Fringilla cœlebs*), several pairs of which were released in Central Park under the direction of Mr. Eugene Schieffiin in 1890, appears not to have survived.

*229. **Carpodacus purpureus** (*Gmel.*). PURPLE FINCH. (517.) —Eastern North America, breeding from northern Minnesota and Long Island northward, and wintering from the Northern States to the Gulf. In the vicinity of New York City the Purple Finch is a rather rare summer resident, a very common migrant, and not common winter resident. It is apparently increasing in numbers during the summer on Long Island (*Dutcher*, MS.).

*230. **Loxia curvirostra minor** (*Brehm*). AMERICAN CROSSBILL. (521.)—Breeds from the Northern States northward and, in the Alleghanies, southward to the Carolinas; in winter wanders irregularly southward, sometimes reaching the Gulf. It is here a regular winter visitant. This erratic species has on several occasions been found breeding south of its regular breeding range.

Such an instance occurred at Riverdale, N. Y., where it was found nesting on April 22, 1874 (*Bicknell*, Bull. N. O. C., IV, 1880, p. 7).

FIG. 19. AMERICAN CROSSBILL.

231. Loxia leucoptera *Gmel.* WHITE-WINGED CROSSBILL. (522.)—This species has much the same distribution as the preceding but does not wander so far south. It is here of more rare and irregular occurrence in winter than the preceding species.

232. Acanthis linaria (*Linn.*). REDPOLL. (528.)—"Northern portions of the Northern Hemisphere, south irregularly in winter, in North America, to the Middle States." This species is here an irregular winter visitant, sometimes occurring in considerable numbers.

233. Acanthis linaria rostrata (*Brehm*). HOLBŒLL'S REDPOLL. (528*b*.)—"Southern Greenland in summer, migrating south, in winter, through Labrador to (sparingly) the northern border of the United States (New England, lower Hudson Valley, northern Illinois, etc.), and west to Manitoba" (*Ridgw.*). Two specimens taken at Sing Sing, N. Y., are the only individuals of this species which have been recorded from this vicinity (*Fisher*, Bull. N. O. C., VIII, 1883, p. 121).

*****234. Spinus tristis** (*Linn.*). AMERICAN GOLDFINCH. (529.) —Eastern North America, breeding from South Carolina to southern Labrador, and wintering from the northern United States to the Gulf. The Goldfinch, Yellowbird, or Thistlebird, is here a common resident.

Fig. 20. American Goldfinch.

*Carduelis carduelis (*Linn.*). European Goldfinch.—
A European species which was introduced into this country at Hoboken, N. J., in 1878. The following year it appeared in Central Park and has since spread over the upper parts of the city where in favorable localities it is not uncommon. It is with us throughout the year. (*Adney*, Auk, III, 1886, p 409).

*235. Spinus pinus (*Wils.*). Pine Siskin ; Pine Finch. (533.)
—North America generally, breeding mostly north of the United States, and wintering as far south as the Gulf. It is here a more or less common fall and winter visitant, and on two occasions has

Fig. 21. Pine Finch.

been found nesting in the Lower Hudson Valley, at Sing Sing, May 25, 1883 (*Fisher*, Bull. N. O. C., VIII, 1883), and at Cornwall-on-Hudson, May 12, 1887 (*Allen*, Auk, IV, 1887, p. 284). (See Group, Gallery, between Cases P and Q.)

236. Plectrophenax nivalis (*Linn.*). SNOWFLAKE; SNOW BUNTING. (534.)—"Northern parts of the Northern Hemisphere, breeding in the Arctic Regions; in North America south in winter into the northern United States, irregularly to Georgia, southern Illinois, and Kansas." On Long Island this bird is an abundant winter resident on the sand-flats near the ocean (*Dutcher*, MS.). In the Lower Hudson Valley it is much less common.

237. Calcarius lapponicus (*Linn.*). LAPLAND LONGSPUR. (536.)—"Northern portions of the Northern Hemisphere, breeding far north; in North America, south in winter to the northern United States, irregularly to the Middle States, accidentally to South Carolina". In this vicinity it is a rare winter resident, and is sometimes found with flocks of the preceding, but is more frequently associated with Horned Larks.

238. Calcarius ornatus (*Towns.*). CHESTNUT-COLLARED LONGSPUR. (538.)—"Interior of North America, from the Saskatchewan Plains south to Texas". A specimen of this western species was taken at Long Island City, February 16, 1889 (*Hendrickson*, Auk, VI, 1889, p. 190).

*****239. Poocætes gramineus** (*Gmel.*). VESPER SPARROW; GRASS FINCH; BAY-WINGED BUNTING. (540.)—North America; breeds from southern Illinois and Virginia northward to New Brunswick and Manitoba, and winters on the Atlantic coast from Virginia southward. This species is here a common summer resident, arriving about April 1, and remaining until the latter part of November.

240. Ammodramus princeps (*Mayn.*). IPSWICH SPARROW. (541.)—Breeds probably on the Atlantic coast from Nova Scotia (Sable Island) northward, winters southward along the coast regularly to Virginia and rarely to Georgia (*Worthington*, Auk, VIII, 1890, p. 211). This species is a common winter resident, confined strictly to the immediate vicinity of the coasts, where it is found from the middle of October to the first of April (*Dutcher*, Auk, III, 1886, p. 441)

*241. **Ammodramus sandwichensis savanna** (*Wils.*). SAVANNA SPARROW. (542*a*. —Eastern North America, breeding from Missouri and northern New Jersey north to Labrador and Hudson Bay, and wintering from southern Illinois and Virginia southward to Cuba and Mexico. This species is here a rare summer resident and abundant migrant, arriving about April 1 and departing in November and December. It breeds at Morristown, N. J. (*Thurber*), and is said to remain throughout the winter in the salt-marshes at Bridgeport, Conn. (*Averill*).

FIG. 22. SAVANNA SPARROW.

242. **Ammodramus savannarum passerinus** (*Wils.*). GRASSHOPPER SPARROW; YELLOW-WINGED SPARROW. (546.)— Eastern North America, breeding from the Gulf States northward to Massachusetts and Minnesota, and wintering from North Carolina to Cuba. In this vicinity it is a common summer resident, arriving about May 1 and remaining until October.

243. **Ammodramus henslowii** (*Aud.*). HENSLOW'S SPARROW. (547.)—Eastern North America, breeding locally from Missouri and Virginia northward to New Hampshire and southern Ontario, and wintering from about the southern limit of its breeding range to the Gulf. In this vicinity Henslow's Sparrow has been found in but few localities where, however, it is apparently not uncommon. It is recorded as breeding at Morristown, N. J. (*Thurber*).

244. **Ammodramus caudacutus** (*Gmel.*). SHARP-TAILED SPARROW. (549.)—Atlantic coast, breeding from South Carolina to New Hampshire, and wintering from North Carolina to Florida. This species is here an abundant resident and, with the exception

of a colony on the Hudson at Piermont, is, so far as known, confined entirely to the salt marshes of our coasts. (See Group, Gallery, between Cases H and I.)

245. Ammodramus caudacutus nelsoni *Allen.* NELSON'S SHARP-TAILED SPARROW. (549*a*.)—Breeds in the marshes of the interior from northern Illinois northward to Dakota and Manitoba; occurs as a migrant on the Atlantic coast, and winters from South Carolina to Texas. This species is known here only as a rather rare fall migrant in the Hudson River Valley, occurring from the latter part of September to the latter part of October.

246. Ammodramus caudacutus subvirgatus *Dwight.* ACADIAN SHARP-TAILED SPARROW. (549*b*.)—"Marshes of southern New Brunswick, Prince Edwards Island and probably Nova Scotia, and southward in migration along the Atlantic coast" (*Dwight*). This bird occurs with the preceding.

247. Ammodramus maritimus (*Wils.*). SEASIDE SPARROW. (550.)—Atlantic coast, breeding from North Carolina to Massachusetts, and wintering from Virginia to Georgia. This is an even more abundant summer resident than the Sharp-tailed Finch and, like it, is confined exclusively to our coasts, with the exception of a colony in the Piermont marshes. (See Group, Gallery, between Cases H and I.)

FIG. 23. SEASIDE SPARROW.

248. Chondestes grammacus (*Say*). LARK SPARROW. (552.) —Interior of North America, eastward to Illinois, breeding from

Texas to Manitoba; accidental on the Atlantic coast. There are two records for this vicinity, Sayville, L. I., August 20, 1879 (*Earle*, Bull. N. O. C., VI, 1881, p. 58) and Schraalenburg, N. J., November 26, 1885 (*Chapman*, Auk, III, 1886, p. 136).

*249. **Zonotrichia leucophrys** (*Forst.*). WHITE-CROWNED SPARROW. (554.)—"Breeding from higher mountain ranges of western United States, Sierra Nevada, Rocky Mountains, and eastward, north of the Great Lakes, to Labrador; in winter, over whole United States, and south into Mexico" (*Ridgw.*). This species occurs here as a rather rare migrant, passing northward in May and returning in October.

FIG. 24. WHITE-CROWNED SPARROW.

*250. **Zonotrichia albicollis** (*Gmel.*). WHITE-THROATED SPARROW. (558.)—Eastern North America, breeding from northern Michigan, and occasionally Massachusetts, northward to Labrador, and wintering from Connecticut to Florida. This species is here an abundant migrant and locally common winter resident. It arrives from the north the latter part of September and remains with us until May.

*251. **Spizella monticola** (*Gmel.*). TREE SPARROW. (559.)— Eastern North America, breeding in Labrabor and the region about Hudson Bay; south in winter, through eastern United States, west to the edge of the Great Plains. With us this bird

FIG. 25. WHITE-THROATED SPARROW.

is an abundant winter resident, arriving from the north about November 1 and remaining until April.

*252. Spizella socialis (*Wils.*). CHIPPING SPARROW; CHIPPY. (560.)—Eastern North America, breeding from the Gulf States to Newfoundland and Great Slave Lake, and wintering in the Gulf States and Mexico. The Chippy is here an abundant summer resident, arriving from the south about April 1 and remaining until November.

*253. Spizella pusilla (*Wils.*). FIELD SPARROW. (563.)—Eastern North America, breeding from southern Illinois and South Carolina to Quebec and Manitoba; winters from Illinois and Virginia southward. With us it is an abundant summer resident, appearing in the spring about April 1 and not departing southward until November and even December. (See Group, Gallery, between Cases C and D.)

*254. Junco hyemalis (*Linn.*). JUNCO; SNOWBIRD. (567.)—North America, breeding from northern Minnesota and northern New York northward, and southward along the summits of the Alleghanies to Virginia; winters southward to the Gulf States. The Junco is our most abundant winter bird. It comes to us from the north late in September and remains until May.

*255. Melospiza fasciata (*Gmel.*). SONG SPARROW. (581.) —Eastern North America, breeding from northern Illinois and Virginia north to Quebec and Manitoba, and wintering from south-

FIG. 26. JUNCO.

ern Illinois and Massachusetts to the Gulf. This species is here an abundant summer and common winter resident. (See Group, Gallery, between Cases O and P.)

256. Melospiza lincolni (*Aud.*). LINCOLN'S SPARROW. (583.) —Eastern North America, breeding from northern Illinois and northern New York northward, and wintering from southern Illinois to Mexico; rare east of the Alleghanies. In this vicinity Lincoln's Sparrow is a rare but regular migrant, passing northward in May and southward in September and October (*Dutcher*, MS.).

*****257. Melospiza georgiana** (*Lath.*). SWAMP SPARROW. (584.) —Eastern North America, breeding from northern Illinois and Pennsylvania northward to Labrador; winters from southern Illinois and northern New Jersey to the Gulf. This bird is an abundant summer resident, especially in the great marshes of the Hackensack, and a rare winter resident. (See Group, Gallery, between Cases O and P.)

*****258. Passerella iliaca** (*Merr.*). FOX SPARROW. (585.)— Breeds from the Magdalen Islands and Manitoba to Alaska, and winters from Virginia southward. This Sparrow occurs as a common spring and fall migrant, passing northward in March and April and southward in October and November.

*259. **Pipilo erythrophthalmus** (*Linn.*). TOWHEE; CHEWINK. (587.)--Eastern North America, breeding from the Lower Mississippi Valley and Georgia northward to Maine, Ontario, and Manitoba. The Chewink is here an abundant summer resident, arriving about April 20 and remaining until late October. (See Group, main floor, opposite Case P.)

*260. **Cardinalis cardinalis** (*Linn.*). CARDINAL. (593.)--Eastern United States, breeding from Florida to Iowa and southern New York; resident throughout its range. The vicinity of New York City is about the northern limit of the Cardinal's range on the Atlantic coast. It is here a not uncommon resident of local distribution. In the Hudson Valley it is not found north of Hastings; it is very rare eastward along the sound, and also on Long Island, but is common in Central Park, New York City, where I have seen nine individuals at one time. (See Group, main floor, opp. Case N.)

*261. **Habia ludoviciana** (*Linn.*). ROSE-BREASTED GROSBEAK. (593.)--Eastern North America, breeding from eastern Kansas, Virginia and the higher altitudes of North Carolina, northward to Maine and Manitoba, wintering in Central and South America. This bird is a common summer resident in the Hudson River Valley, arriving about May 1 and remaining until October. On Long Island it is a rare summer resident (*Dutcher*, MS.). (See Group, main floor, Alcove N.)

*262. **Guiraca cærulea** (*Linn.*). BLUE GROSBEAK. (597.)--United States, breeding from about latitude 38° southward into Mexico, and wintering south of our limits. There are several records of this bird's occurrence in this vicinity where, of course, it is only an accidental visitor. It has been taken at Carnarsie, (L. I., May, 1843 (*Dutcher*, Auk, V, 1893, p 276); Morristown, N. J. (*Thurber*, True Democratic Banner, newspaper, Nov. 17, 1889); Snake Hill, N. J. (*Bicknell*, Bull. N. O. C., III, 1878, p 132), and Manhattan Island (*DeKay*, Birds, N. Y., p. 146).

Passerina ciris (*Linn.*). PAINTED BUNTING. (601.)--Breeds from the Gulf States northward to Kansas, southern Illinois and North Carolina. The capture of several specimens of this bird in this vicinity has been recorded (*Bicknell*, Bull. N. O. C., III, 1878, p. 132). It is probable that they were escaped cage-birds.

*263. **Passerina cyanea** (*Linn.*). INDIGO BUNTING. (598.)--

Eastern United States, breeding as far north as Minnesota and
Nova Scotia, and wintering in Central America This species is
a common summer resident in this vicinity, arriving about May 1
and remaining until October 1.

264. Spiza americana (*Gmel.*). DICKCISSEL; BLACK-THROAT-
ED BUNTING. (604.)—Eastern United States, mostly in the
Mississippi Valley, breeding from Texas to Minnesota, and wintering in Central and South America; breeds east of the Alleghanies
now only rarely and locally. About forty years ago this bird was
evidently a regular and not uncommon summer resident in this
vicinity (see *Giraud, Chapman, apud Galbraith*, Auk, VIII, 1891, p.
395), but it occurs now only rarely and irregularly. Recent records
are: Miller's Place, L. I , September 29 and October 10 (*Dutcher*,
Auk, VI, 1889, p. 13), and Blithewood, L. I., August 25 (*Johnson*,
Auk, VIII, 1891, p. 116).

Family TANAGRIDÆ.—TANAGERS.

265. Piranga ludoviciana (*Wils.*). LOUISIANA TANAGER.
(607.)—Western North America north to British Columbia. The
only record of the occurrence of this western species in this vicinity
is that of a young male taken at Fort Montgomery, N Y , December 21, 1881 (*Mearns*, Auk, VII, 1890, p. 55).

*****266. Piranga erythromelas** *Vieill*. SCARLET TANAGER.
(608.)—Eastern North America, breeding from southern Illinois
and Virginia to Manitoba and New Brunswick, and wintering in
Central and northern South America. With us it is a common
summer resident, arriving early in May and remaining until about
October 1. (See Group, Gallery, between Cases S and T.)

*****267. Piranga rubra** (*Linn.*). SUMMER TANAGER. (610.)—
Eastern United States, breeding from Florida to southern New
Jersey, wandering casually to Nova Scotia, and wintering in Cen-
tral and South America. This species is of rare and irregular
occurrence in this vicinity. (*Hendrickson*, Auk, I, 1885, p 290;
Dutcher, ibid, III, 1886, p 412; V, 1888, p. 181 ; *Mearns, ibid.,*
VII, 1890, p. 55.)

Family HIRUNDINIDÆ. —SWALLOWS.

268 Progne subis (*Linn.*). PURPLE MARTIN (611.)—
North America, north to Newfoundland and the Saskatchewan,
breeding throughout its range, and wintering in Central and South

America. This bird breeds in colonies and is of local distribution during the breeding season. It was formerly not uncommon in the vicinity of New York City but the English Sparrows have taken possession of its nesting-houses and at present it is found in but few places.

269. Petrochelidon lunifrons (*Say*). CLIFF SWALLOW; EAVE SWALLOW. (612.)—North America, north to Labrador and, in the interior, to the Arctic Ocean, breeding throughout its range and wintering in the tropics. Like most of the Swallows it nests in colonies, and in this region generally places its mud nests beneath the projecting eaves of a barn. It appears to be less common during the summer than it was ten or more years ago, but is a common migrant, particularly in the fall. According to Dr. Mearns, it arrives as early as April 16. (See Group, main floor, between Cases Q and R.)

*270. **Chelidon erythrogaster** (*Bodd.*). BARN SWALLOW. (613.)—North America, north to Greenland and Alaska, breeding throughout the greater part of its range, and wintering as far south as southern Brazil. With us the Barn Swallow is a common summer and an abundant fall migrant. It arrives about April 20 and remains until October 1.

*271. **Tachycineta bicolor** (*Vieill.*). TREE SWALLOW. (614.) —North America, north to Labrador and Alaska, breeding locally throughout its range, and wintering from South Carolina southward. In this vicinity it arrives from the south early in April. There are a few recorded instances of its breeding near New York City but, generally speaking, the species passes onward to more distant nesting grounds. July 1 they begin to return from the north, making their home in the marshes of the Hackensack, where, by July 20, they may be found in countless numbers. In the morning they leave their roosts in the 'cat-tails' and fly out over the adjoining country to feed. At night they return. Their numbers increase until about September 1, then decrease, and by October 20 only a few stragglers remain.

*272. **Clivicola riparia** (*Linn.*). BANK SWALLOW. (616.)— North America, north to Labrador and Alaska, breeding locally throughout its range, and wintering as far south as Brazil. It is here a common summer resident, breeding in colonies where the conditions are favorable. It arrives about May 1 and remains until October. (See Group, main floor, between Cases R and S.)

273. Stelgidopteryx serripennis (*Aud.*). ROUGH-WINGED SWALLOW. (617.)—North America, breeding as far north as British Columbia, Minnesota and Connecticut, and wintering in the tropics. This Swallow is locally common in the Lower Hudson River Valley, at Riverdale (*Bicknell*), Hastings-on-the-Hudson (*Rowley*), Sing Sing (*Fisher*); at Highland Falls, which seems to be near the northern limit of its range in the Hudson Valley, it is a rare summer resident (*Mearns*). I have seen it near Ramapo, N. Y., and with Dr. J. Dwight, Jr., found a small colony breeding at Port Jervis, N. Y. It breeds near New Haven, Connecticut, in small numbers, and is rare as far north as Hartford (*Sage*). On Long Island it is of rare and irregular occurrence (*Dutcher*)

Family AMPELIDÆ.—WAXWINGS, ETC.

274. Ampelis garrulus *Linn.* BOHEMIAN WAXWING. (618.)—Northern parts of the Northern Hemisphere; in North America, south in winter, irregularly, to the northern United States. This species occurs here only as an exceedingly rare and irregular winter visitant. There are no recent records.

*****275. Ampelis cedrorum** (*Vieill.*). CEDAR WAXWING; CEDARBIRD. (619.)—North America, breeding from Virginia and the Highlands of South Carolina north to Labrador; winters from the northern United States to Central America. This bird is here a common summer resident and, in favorable localities, a not uncommon winter resident

Family LANIIDÆ.—SHRIKES.

*****276. Lanius borealis** *Vieill.* NORTHERN SHRIKE; BUTCHERBIRD. (621.)—Breeds in the interior in the far north (Fort Anderson, *Macfarlane*), and migrates southward in winter as far as Kan-

FIG. 27. NORTHERN SHRIKE.

sas and Washington, D. C. This species is here a more or less regular but rather uncommon winter resident.

277 Lanius ludovicianus *Linn.* LOGGERHEAD SHRIKE. (622.)—Eastern North America west to the edge of the Plains; breeds, east of the Alleghanies, as far north as Virginia, west of the Alleghanies breeds northward to the Great Lakes and eastward through Central New York to Vermont and Maine. The Loggerhead Shrike is found here as a very rare migrant during the latter part of August and in September. It has been known to breed but once, at Sing Sing, N. Y., where a fledgeling was taken June 16, 1877 (*Fisher*, Bull. N. O. C., IV, 1879, p. 61).

Family VIREONIDÆ.—VIREOS.

*278. Vireo olivaceus (*Linn.*). RED-EYED VIREO. (624.)— Eastern North America, westward to British Columbia, breeding from the Gulf States to Labrador and Manitoba, and wintering in Central and South America. This is one of our abundant summer residents. It arrives from the south about May 8, and remains until October. (See Group, Gallery, between Cases R and S.)

279. Vireo philadelphicus (*Cass.*). PHILADELPHIA VIREO. (626.)—Eastern North America, breeding in Manitoba, Maine, and probably north to Labrador, and wintering in the tropics. With us this Vireo occurs only as a very rare migrant.

*280. Vireo gilvus (*Vieill.*). WARBLING VIREO. (627.)— North America, breeding as far north as the Hudson Bay region and wintering in the tropics. It is here a common summer resident of local distribution, arriving early in May. (See Group, Gallery, between Cases L and M.)

*281. Vireo flavifrons *Vieill.* YELLOW-THROATED VIREO. (628.)—Eastern North America, breeding from Florida to Newfoundland and Manitoba, and wintering in the tropics. Here a common summer resident, arriving about May 7 and remaining until the latter part of September.

282. Vireo solitarius (*Wils.*). BLUE-HEADED VIREO. (629.) —Eastern North America, breeding from Connecticut (and southward along the crests of the Alleghanies) northward to New Brunswick and Manitoba, and wintering from Florida southward. It is here a not uncommon migrant, passing northward during the latter part of April and first part of May, and returning late in September.

*283. Vireo noveboracensis (*Gmel.*). WHITE-EYED VIREO. (631.)—Eastern United States, breeding from Florida to New Hampshire and Minnesota, and wintering from Florida southward. This species is a common summer resident about New York City. It reaches us from the south about May 7, and remains until early October. See Group, Gallery, between Cases R and S.)

Family MNIOTILTIDÆ.—WOOD-WARBLERS.

*284. Mniotilta varia (*Linn.*). BLACK AND WHITE WARBLER. (636.)—Eastern North America, breeding from the Southern States north to Fort Simpson, and wintering from Florida southward. The Black and White Warbler, or, as it is sometimes called, the Black and White Creeper, is here a tolerably common summer resident and common migrant. It appears the latter part of April and is with us until the first part of October. (See Group, Gallery, between Cases M and N.)

285. Protonotaria citrea (*Bodd.*). PROTHONOTARY WARBLER. (637.)—Eastern North America, breeding from the Gulf States to southern Illinois and Virginia, and wintering in the tropics. Its occurrence near New York City is accidental; there is but one record, viz., a male shot at Jamaica, L. I. (*Dutcher*, Auk, X, 1893, p. 276). The same author has recorded a specimen which struck the Montauk Point Lighthouse, August 27, 1886 (*ibid.*, V, 1888, p. 182)

*286. Helmitherus vermivorus (*Gmel.*). WORM-EATING WARBLER. (639.)—Eastern United States, breeding from the Gulf States north to southern Illinois and southern Connecticut, and wintering in the tropics. This bird is one of our rarer summer residents, though it is not uncommon some years in the early fall migration. In the Hudson River Valley it is regularly found as far north as Highland Falls (*Mearns*) and occurs at Fishkill (*Stearns*). In Connecticut it breeds at Saybrook and New Haven, but is not common, and at Portland it has been taken only twice (*Sage*). On Long Island it is considered exceedingly rare (*Dutcher*).

*287. Helminthophila pinus (*Linn.*). BLUE-WINGED WARBLER. (641.)—Eastern United States, breeding as far north as southern Minnesota and Connecticut, and wintering in the tropics.

This species arrives early in May and remains until September 1. It is a common summer resident of the Lower Hudson Valley, at least as far north as Highland Falls (*Mearns*). In Connecticut it is common at Saybrook and New Haven, but is rare as far north as Portland where but one or two pairs breed each season (*Sage*). On Long Island it is known to breed only along the north shore, where it is probably not uncommon in favorable localities. (See Group, Gallery, between Cases M and N.)

Brewster's Warbler (*Helminthophila leucobronchialis*) with us is a rare but regular summer resident in northern New Jersey, the Lower Hudson Valley and southern Connecticut, but has been taken only once on Long Island (*Howell*). Specimens have been recorded from Morristown (*Thurber*), Maplewood (*Riker*), and Englewood, N. J., where it has been found nesting (*Chapman*, Auk, IV, 1887, p. 348; IX, 1892, p. 302). Farther north in the Hudson Valley it has been found at Nyack (*Bicknell*), and at Sing Sing five specimens have been secured (*Fisher*, Bull. N. O. C, IV, 1879, p. 234; VI, 1881, p. 245; Auk, II, 1885, p. 378). In the Lower Connecticut Valley this bird seems to be more frequent than in any other part of its range. It has been found at Saybrook, Seymour, New Haven, Portland, and other localities, the principal records being as follows: *Eames*, Auk, V, 1888, p. 427; VI, 1889, p. 305; *Bishop*, ibid., VI, 1889, p. 192; *Sage*, ibid., X, 1893, p. 208. Probably not more than one-third of all the specimens recorded are *typical leucobronchialis*, the remaining two-thirds presenting every stage of intergradation between this bird and typical *H. pinus*.

Lawrence's Warbler (*Helminthophila lawrencei*) is a much rarer bird than the preceding. There are records for only three typical specimens from the immediate vicinity of New York City, viz., Chatham, N. J. (*Herrick*), Hoboken, N. J. (*Lawrence*), and Rye, N. Y. (*Vorhees*, Auk, V, 1888, p. 427).

Five specimens have been recorded from Connecticut, the details of their capture being given under the references cited for *H. leucobronchialis*.

The status of both Brewster's and Lawrence's Warbler is still unsettled. They are generally considered to be hybrids between *H. pinus* and *H. chrysoptera*, and it has also been suggested that dichromatism may play a part in producing their coloration. Their relationship will be found discussed under the following references: *Brewster*, Bull. N. O. C., VI, 1881, p. 218; *Ridgway*, Auk, II, 1885, p. 359; Manual N. A. Birds, 1887, p. 486.

*288. **Helminthophila chrysoptera** (*Linn*). GOLDEN-WINGED WARBLER. (642.)—Eastern North America, breeding from Indiana and northern New Jersey north to Michigan, southern Ontario, and Vermont, south along the coast of the Alleghanies to South Carolina; winters in Central America. In the immediate vicinity of New York City this bird occurs as a rather rare spring migrant but in the early southward migration, in August, it is sometimes not uncommon. It has been found nesting at Nyack, N. Y. (*Brownell*), and probably breeds regularly from that point northward.

*289. **Helminthophila ruficapilla** (*Wils.*). NASHVILLE WARBLER. (645.)—Eastern North America, breeding from northern Illinois and Connecticut northward to Labrador and the Fur Countries. This species is here a tolerably common migrant and a rare summer resident as far south as Highland Falls. It arrives about May 10 and returns on its southward journey during late August, the last migrants being seen about September 25.

290. **Helminthophila celata** (*Say*). ORANGE-CROWNED WARBLER. (646.)—Breeds in the interior of British Columbia, as far north as the "Yukon and Mackenzie River districts, and southward through the Rocky Mountains, wintering in the South Atlantic and Gulf States and Mexico". This Warbler occurs here as an exceedingly rare migrant. There are records of only six specimens, all but one of which occurred in the fall. (See *Howell*, Auk, X, 1893, p. 91.)

291. **Helminthophila peregrina** (*Wils*). TENNESSEE WARBLER. (647.)—Eastern North America, breeding from Minnesota, northern New York and New Brunswick northward, and wintering in Central America. With us this bird is a rather rare spring migrant, but is sometimes not uncommon in the fall. It passes northward early in May and returns on its southern journey in September.

*292. **Compsothlypis americana** (*Linn.*). PARULA WARBLER. (648.)—Eastern North America, breeding from the Gulf States northward to Anticosti, and wintering from Florida southward. The Parula Warbler is here a more or less abundant migrant, and locally common summer resident. It arrives from the south about May 7 and the last individuals are observed in early October.

*293. **Dendroica tigrina** (*Gmel*). CAPE MAY WARBLER. (650.)

—Eastern North America, breeding from northern New England north to Hudson Bay, and wintering in the tropics. This is one of our rarest spring migrants, passing northward about May 15. In the fall migration immature birds are sometimes not uncommon.

*294. **Dendroica æstiva** (*Gmel.*). YELLOW WARBLER. (652.) —North America, except southwestern States, breeding northward to the Arctic Regions and wintering as far south as northern South America. This bird is one of our common summer residents. It arrives from the south about May 5 and remains until September. (See Group, Gallery, between Cases N and O.)

*295. **Dendroica cærulescens** (*Gmel.*). BLACK-THROATED BLUE WARBLER. (654.)—Eastern North America, breeding from northern Minnesota (probably) and Connecticut (rarely) northward to Labrador, and south along the crest of the Alleghanies to Georgia. It is one of our common migrant Warblers, passing northward early in May and returning in September.

FIG. 28. MYRTLE WARBLER.

*296. **Dendroica coronata** (*Linn.*). MYRTLE WARBLER; YELLOW-RUMPED WARBLER. (655.)—Eastern North America, breeding from northern Minnesota and northern New England northward, and wintering from the Middle States southward. This species is an abundant migrant in our vicinity and in favorable localities where food is abundant, it passes the whole winter. Migrants begin to arrive in early April, and the southward migration takes place during the latter part of September and October.

*297. **Dendroica maculosa** (*Gmel.*). MAGNOLIA WARBLER. (657.)—Eastern North America, breeding from northern Michigan and northern New England to Hudson Bay, and southward along the Alleghanies to Pennsylvania, and wintering in Central America. In this vicinity it is a common migrant, passing northward early in May and returning late in August and in September.

298. **Dendroica cærulea** (*Wils.*). CERULEAN WARBLER. (658.)—Breeds in the Mississippi Valley as far north as Minnesota, and eastward as far as Lockport, N. Y. (*Davison*), and winters in the tropics. Its occurrence here is accidental and there are but two records of its capture, one of a male taken in Kings County, L. I. (*Dutcher*, Auk, X, 1893, p. 277), and one of a male taken at

Highland Falls, May 17, 1875 (*Mearns*, Birds Hudson Highlands p. 154).

*299. **Dendroica pensylvanica** (*Linn.*). CHESTNUT-SIDED WARBLER. (659.)—Eastern North America, breeding from central Illinois and northern New Jersey north to Manitoba and Newfoundland, and southward along the crest of the Alleghanies to South Carolina. With us it is a common migrant, and, in northern New Jersey, a rare summer resident. It arrives early in May, and the return migration occurs between August 10 and October 1.

*300. **Dendroica castanea** (*Wils.*). BAY-BREASTED WARBLER. (660. — Eastern Northern America, breeding from northern Michigan and northern New England northward to Hudson Bay and Labrador, and wintering in Central America. As a rule the Bay-breasted is one of our rarest transient Warblers but during some seasons it is found in numbers. It passes northward about the middle of May and returns in September.

*301. **Dendroica striata** (*Forst.*). BLACKPOLL WARBLER. (661.)—"Eastern North America to the Rocky Mountains, north to Greenland, the Barren Grounds, and Alaska, breeding from northern New England northward. South in winter to northern South America." The Blackpoll is one of our most abundant migrants, and is the last of the Warblers to reach us in the spring. It passes northward from May 20 to 30 and returns on its southern journey in September.

FIG. 29. BLACKPOLL WARBLER.

*302. **Dendroica blackburniæ** (*Gmel.*). BLACKBURNIAN WARBLER. (662.)—Eastern North America, breeding from northern Minnesota and southern Maine northward to Labrador, and southward along the Alleghanies to South Carolina, and wintering in the tropics. In this vicinity it is a rather uncommon spring migrant, passing northward during the first half of May, but is not uncommon some years during its return migration in September.

303. **Dendroica dominica** (*Linn.*). YELLOW-THROATED WARBLER. (663.)—Southern United States, breeding as far north as Virginia, and wintering from Florida southward. There is but one record of the occurrence of this southern species near New York City. It is based on the capture of a male in Kings County, L. I. (*Dutcher*, Auk, X, 1893, p. 277)

*304. **Dendroica virens** (*Gmel.*). BLACK-THROATED GREEN
WARBLER. (667.)—Eastern North America, breeding from northern
Illinois and Connecticut northward to Hudson Bay and southward
along the Alleghanies to South Carolina. In the immediate
vicinity of New York City this bird is found only as a migrant,
arriving from the south late in April and returning about the
middle of August. It is known to breed at Highland Falls, N. Y.
(*Mearns*), Bridgeport, Conn. (*Averill*), and Millers Place, L. I.
(*Dutcher*, MS.).

*305. **Dendroica vigorsii** (*Aud.*). PINE WARBLER. (671.)—
Eastern North America, breeding from Hayti (?), the Bahamas and
Florida north to Manitoba and Maine, and wintering from southern
Illinois and North Carolina southward. This Warbler is of local
distribution in this vicinity. In northern New Jersey, the Lower
Hudson Valley and southern Connecticut it occurs only as a rare
migrant, but on certain parts of Long Island, where the scrub
pines afford it congenial surroundings, it is not uncommon and
breeds.

306. **Dendroica palmarum** (*Gmel.*). PALM WARBLER. (672.)
—Breeds in the interior of British America north of Manitoba
and west of Hudson Bay, migrates southward through the Mississippi
Valley, and winters in the South Atlantic and Gulf States, West
Indies, and Mexico; casual in the North Atlantic States. This
species is of rare occurrence here. One specimen was taken at
Sing Sing, N. Y., April 29, 1882 (*Fisher*, Bull. N. O. C., VII, 1882,
p. 249), two at Riverdale, N. Y., in the spring of 1877 (*Bicknell*,
Bull. N. O. C., V, 1880, p. 182), and one struck the Fire Island
Lighthouse September 23, 1887 (*Dutcher*, Auk, V, 1888, p. 182).

*307. **Dendroica palmarum hypochrysea** *Ridgw.* YELLOW
PALM WARBLER; YELLOW REDPOLL. (672a.)—Breeds from Nova
Scotia northward east of Hudson Bay and migrates southward
through the Atlantic States to winter in the Gulf States. This
bird is here a common migrant arriving from the south about April
10, and returning late in September and in October.

308. **Dendroica discolor** (*Vieill.*). PRAIRIE WARBLER. (673.)
—Breeds from Florida to Michigan and Massachusetts and winters
from southern Florida southward. The distribution of the Prairie
Warbler in this vicinity is much like that of the Pine Warbler.
It is rare in northern New Jersey and the Lower Hudson Valley,

where, however, it has been found breeding once (Highland Falls, *Mearns*), but is not uncommon on some parts of Long Island. At Bridgeport, Conn., it is a common migrant and may breed (*Averill*). (See Group, Gallery, between Cases E and F.)

*309 **Seiurus aurocapillus** (*Linn.*). OVENBIRD. (674.)—Eastern North America, breeding from Kansas and Virginia northward to Manitoba and Labrador, southward along the Alleghanies to South Carolina; winters from Florida southward. The Ovenbird is one of our abundant summer residents arriving about May 1 and remaining until the middle of October. (See Group, Gallery, between Cases G and H.)

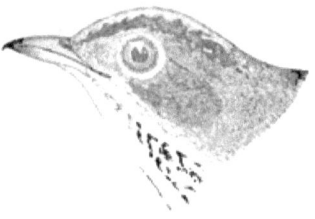

FIG. 30. OVENBIRD.

*310. **Seiurus noveboracensis** (*Gmel.*). WATER-THRUSH. (675.)—Eastern United States, breeding from northern Illinois and Massachusetts northward and wintering from the Gulf States to northern South America. With us this species is a common migrant, passing northward during May and returning about September 1.

311. **Seiurus noveboracensis notabilis** (*Grinn.*). GRINNELL'S WATER-THRUSH. (675*a*.)—" United States, from Illinois westward to California, and north into British America"; eastward during the migrations to Virginia and the South Atlantic States, and wintering from the Gulf States to northern South America. This western species is of a casual occurrence here It has been recorded only from Raritan, N. J., May 30, 1889 (*Southwick*, Auk, IX, 1892, p. 303).

*312 **Seiurus motacilla** (*Vieill.*). LOUISIANA WATER-THRUSH. (676.)—Eastern United States, breeding as far north as Minnesota and Connecticut and wintering in the tropics. It is a common summer resident in the Lower Hudson Valley, has been found as far north as Lake George (*Fisher*), and is not uncommon in the Lower Connecticut Valley. There are two records for Massachusetts and two for Rhode Island. On Long Island it is very rare (*Dutcher*). (See Group, Gallery, between Cases Q and R).

*313. **Geothlypis formosa** (*Wils.*). KENTUCKY WARBLER. (677.)—Eastern United States, breeding from the Gulf States to Iowa and Connecticut, and wintering in Central America. This

PLATE III. LOUISIANA WATER-THRUSH.
(From Group in American Museum of Natural History.)

FIG. 31. KENTUCKY WARBLER.

is a common summer resident on the banks of the Lower Hudson River and has been recorded from Fort Lee and Riverdale (*Bicknell*), Englewood (*Chapman*), and Sing Sing (*Fisher*), beyond which point it is as yet unknown. In Connecticut there are but three records, viz., at Suffield where a male was taken August 16, 1876 (*Merriam*), at Greenwich, where a pair and a fledgeling were seen and the male taken July 10, 1892 (*Vorhees*, Auk, X, 1893, p. 86), and at West Stratford, where a male was shot May 30, 1888 (*Lucas*, Orn. and Oöl., XIV, 1889, p. 62). On Long Island it is very rare, there being but one recent record of its occurrence (*Dutcher*).

314. **Geothlypis agilis** (*Wils.*). CONNECTICUT WARBLER. (678.)—Eastern North America, nesting, as far as known, in Manitoba and wintering in northern South America. This species is an exceedingly rare spring migrant east of the Alleghanies, and I know of no record of its occurrence here at that season; in the fall, however, it is not uncommon, and sometimes is abundant, arriving as early as September 3 and remaining until the latter part of the month.

315. **Geothlypis philadelphia** (*Wils.*). MOURNING WARBLER. (679.)—Eastern North America, breeding from eastern Nebraska, northern New York and Nova Scotia northward, and southward along the Alleghanies to Pennsylvania. This species is one of our rarest Warblers; it passes northward during the latter half of May.

*316. **Geothlypis trichas** (*Linn.*). MARYLAND YELLOW-THROAT. (681.)—Eastern North America, west to the Plains, breeding from the Gulf States to Manitoba and Labrador, and wintering from the Gulf States southward. This is one of our most abundant summer residents. It arrives about May 5 and remains until October. (See Group, Gallery, between Cases N and O.)

*317. **Icteria virens** (*Linn.*). YELLOW-BREASTED CHAT. (683.) —Eastern United States, breeding as far north as southern Minnesota and Massachusetts, and wintering in Central America. The Chat is here a common summer resident, arriving about May 5 and remaining until September.

*318. **Sylvania mitrata** (*Gmel.*). HOODED WARBLER. (684.)
—Eastern United States, breeding as far north as southern Michigan and southern Connecticut, and wintering in Central America. The Hooded Warbler is here near the northern limit of its range. At Englewood, N. J., it is an abundant summer resident, arriving about May 5 and remaining until the middle of September. At Riverdale, N. J., it is locally common (*Bicknell*), at Sing Sing it is not common (*Fisher*), but at Highland Falls it is "very common" (*Mearns*). It has been taken at Fishkill, the most northern point in the Hudson River Valley from which it has been recorded. In Connecticut it is common at Saybrook and New Haven but is rare north of these points (*Sage*). In Massachusetts it has been found only twice. On Long Island it is, as far as known, very rare.

*319. **Sylvania pusilla** (*Wils*). WILSON'S WARBLER. (685.)
—North America, breeding from British Columbia, Minnesota and Nova Scotia northward and wintering in Central America. This bird is here a rare spring migrant, passing northward from the 12th to the 30th of May, but is not uncommon at times during its return journey, which takes place between August 15 and September 15.

*320. **Sylvania canadensis** (*Linn*). CANADIAN WARBLER. (686.)—Eastern North America, breeding from northern Michigan and Massachusetts to Manitoba and Labrador, and wintering in Central and South America. This is one of our common migrants, passing north from May 10 to June 10 and returning between August 5 and September 10.

*321. **Setophaga ruticilla** (*Linn.*) AMERICAN REDSTART. (687.)—North America, breeding from Kansas and North Carolina north to Labrador and Fort Simpson, and wintering in the West Indies, Central America and northern South America. The Redstart is a common summer resident of our woodland; it arrives about May 5 and remains until early October. (See Group, Gallery, between Cases N and O.)

Family MOTACILLIDÆ.—WAGTAILS.

*322. **Anthus pensilvanicus** (*Lath.*). AMERICAN PIPIT; TITLARK (697.)—"North America at large, breeding in the higher parts of the Rocky Mountains and sub-arctic districts and wintering in the Gulf States, Mexico and Central America". The Titlark is a generally common, and along our coasts, an abundant migrant. It travels northward from the latter part of March to early May and returns on its southern journey during October and November.

Family TROGLODYTIDÆ.—WRENS, THRASHERS, ETC.

*323. **Mimus polyglottos** (*Linn.*). MOCKINGBIRD. (703.)—
Breeds from the Bahamas and Mexico to southern Illinois and
northern New Jersey, rarely to Massachusetts, and winters from
North Carolina southward. The Mockingbird is of exceedingly
rare occurrence in this vicinity and doubtless many of the specimens reported are escaped cage-birds. It has, however, been
found breeding at a number of localities, and at Tenafly, N. J., a
pair returned to the same locality for a number of years (Auk, VI,
1889, p. 305). On several occasions Mockingbirds have been found
here during the winter and have shown their ability to withstand
our coldest weather as long as they could obtain an abundance of
food. Probably these birds were escaped cage-birds in which the
instinct of migration had never been developed.

*324. **Galeoscoptes carolinensis** (*Linn*) CATBIRD (704.)
—North America, breeding in the eastern United States from the
Gulf States to New Brunswick and northwestward to the Saskat-
chewan and British Columbia; winters from Florida southward.
This species is an abundant summer resident, arriving about May
3 and remaining until October 20. (See Group, Gallery, between
Cases C and D.)

*325. **Harporhynchus rufus** (*Linn.*). BROWN THRASHER.
(705.)—Eastern North America, breeding from the Gulf States to
Manitoba, Maine and Montreal, and wintering from the Gulf States
southward. The Brown Thrasher or Brown "Thrush", as it is
generally but incorrectly called, is a common summer resident,
appearing about April 20 and remaining until the middle of October. (See Group, main floor, between Cases K and L.)

*326. **Thryothorus ludovicianus** (*Lath.*). CAROLINA WREN.
(718.)—Eastern United States, breeding from the Gulf States to
southern Iowa, northern Illinois, and southern Connecticut; resident, except at the northern limit of its range. Generally speaking the Carolina Wren is a rather rare bird in this vicinity but on
the eastern slope of the Palisades, as far north as Piermont, it is
common during the summer (*Chapman*, Auk, X, 1893, p. 87).
It has been found on Long Island in the winter (*Dutcher*, MS.).

*327. **Troglodytes aëdon** (*Vieill.*). HOUSE WREN. (721.)—
Eastern North America, breeding as far north as Manitoba, Mon-

FIG. 32. CAROLINA WREN.

treal and Maine, and wintering from South Carolina southward. This common and familiar species comes to us about May 1 and remains until October.

*328. **Troglodytes hiemalis** (*Vieill.*). WINTER WREN. (722.) —Eastern North America, breeding from the Northern States northward, and southward along the Alleghanies to North Carolina; winters from Massachusetts and Illinois to Florida. Just before the House Wren leaves us, or about October 1, the Winter Wren comes from the north and is not uncommon until the House Wren returns in May.

FIG. 33. WINTER WREN.

329. Cistothorus stellaris (*Licht.*). SHORT-BILLED MARSH WREN. (624.)—Eastern North America, breeding as far north as Manitoba and Massachusetts, and wintering from the Gulf States southward. This species is here a rare summer resident of local distribution.

330. Cistothorus palustris (*Wils.*). LONG-BILLED MARSH WREN. (625.)—Eastern North America, breeding from the Gulf States to Manitoba and Massachusetts, and wintering from the Gulf States southward. This abundant inhabitant of our reedy marshes arrives in May and remains until October.

Family CERTHIIDÆ.—CREEPERS.

*****331. Certhia familiaris americana** (*Bonap.*). BROWN CREEPER. (726.)—Eastern North America, breeding from Minnesota and Maine northward, migrating south in winter as far as the Gulf States. The Creeper is here a tolerably common winter resident, arriving from the north about October 1 and remaining until April.

Family PARIDÆ.—NUTHATCHES AND TITS.

*****332. Sitta carolinensis** *Lath.* WHITE-BREASTED NUTHATCH. (727.)—Eastern North America, breeding from the Gulf States to Minnesota and New Brunswick; generally resident throughout its range. This species is here a common resident.

*****333. Sitta canadensis** *Linn.* RED-BREASTED NUTHATCH. (728.)— North America, breeding from Manitoba and Maine northward, and southward along the Alleghanies to Virginia; winters from about the southern limit of its breeding range to the Gulf States. This bird is sometimes common from the later part of August to October and is also a rare winter resident.

FIG. 34. RED-BREASTED NUTHATCH.

334. Parus bicolor (*Linn.*). TUFTED TITMOUSE. (731.)— Eastern United States, breeding from the Gulf States to southern Iowa and northern New Jersey; resident throughout its breeding range. This bird is resident and breeds as far north as Orange, N. J. (*Riker*), and Staten Island, N. Y. (*Hollick*). Beyond these points it occurs only irregularly and rarely. It has been observed on several occasions at Englewood, N. J. (*Chapman*), and at Riverdale, N. Y. (*Bicknell*), the most northern records, I believe, for the

Hudson River Valley. There are few records for Connecticut, and although Giraud leads us to believe it was not uncommon and bred on Long Island when he wrote, it is now unknown there.

*335. **Parus atricapillus** (*Linn.*). CHICKADEE. (735.)—Eastern North America, breeding from southern Illinois and Pennsylvania northward to Labrador, and southward along the Alleghanies to North Carolina; in winter migrates a short distance below the southern limit of its breeding range. The Chickadee is here a common resident, but is more numerous during its migration in October than at other times.

336. **Parus carolinensis** *Aud.* CAROLINA CHICKADEE. (736.)— "Southeastern United States, north to New Jersey and Illinois"; resident from Washington southward. This species reaches the southern limit of our district at Princeton, N. J., where, according to Mr. W. E. D. Scott, it is a regular summer resident, while *P. atricapillus* is found there only in the winter (*Scott*, TheCountry, I, 1878, p. 354).

FIG. 35. CHICKADEE.

Family SYLVIIDÆ.—KINGLETS AND GNATCATCHERS.

*337. **Regulus satrapa** *Licht.* GOLDEN-CROWNED KINGLET. (748.)—North America, breeding from the northern United States northward, and southward along the Rockies into Mexico, and in the Alleghanies to North Carolina; winters from the southern limit of its breeding range to the Gulf States. This species is a common winter resident in favorable localities; it arrives from the north about October 1 and remains until May.

*338. **Regulus calendula** (*Linn.*). RUBY-CROWNED KINGLET. (749.)—North America; breeds from the northern border of the United States northward, and winters from South Carolina southward into Mexico. This species is with us a common spring, and an abundant fall migrant, arriving from the south about the middle of April and returning late in September.

FIG. 36. GOLDEN-CROWNED KINGLET.

339. Polioptila cærulea *(Linn.)*. BLUE-GRAY GNATCATCHER. (751.)—Eastern United States, breeding from the Gulf States to northern Illinois, southern Ontario, and northern New Jersey, and wandering rarely to Minnesota and Maine; winters from Florida southward. There are numerous records of capture of this southern species in the vicinity of New York City, but it is not known to occur regularly nearer than Princeton, N. J., where it arrives from "April 25 to May 1" (*Scott*, The Country, I, 1878, p. 354).

Family TURDIDÆ.—THRUSHES, BLUEBIRDS, ETC.

*340. **Turdus mustelinus** *Gmel.* WOOD THRUSH. (755.)— Eastern United States, breeding as far north as Minnesota and northern Maine, and wintering in Central America. The Wood Thrush is an abundant summer resident, arriving about May 1 and remaining until early October. It may rightly claim the rank of the most gifted of our summer songsters. (See Group, main floor, between Cases M and N.)

*341. **Turdus fuscescens** *Steph.* WILSON'S THRUSH. (756.)— Eastern North America, breeding from northern Illinois and Pennsylvania to Manitoba and Newfoundland, and southward along the Alleghanies to North Carolina. Wilson's Thrush, or the Veery, as it is better called, is a common summer resident, arriving about May 1 and remaining until September. (See Group, Gallery, between Cases L and M.)

— 84 —

342. **Turdus aliciæ** *Baird.* GRAY-CHEEKED THRUSH. (757.) — North America, breeding in Labrador and northwestward to Alaska, and migrating through eastern North America to Central America. This bird is a common migrant, passing northward in May and southward in September and October.

343. **Turdus aliciæ bicknelli** (*Ridgw.*). BICKNELL'S THRUSH. (757a)—Breeds in the higher parts of the Catskills and northward to the White Mountains and Nova Scotia; winters in the tropics. So far as records go, this is a rather rare migrant, occurring in May and September and October, but careful search will doubtless show it is more common than is generally supposed.

*344. **Turdus ustulatus swainsonii** (*Cab.*). OLIVE-BACKED THRUSH. (758.)—Breeds from Manitoba and New Brunswick to Alaska and Labrador, and southward in the Rocky Mountains, and along the Alleghanies to Pennsylvania. The Olive-backed Thrush is a common migrant in this vicinity. It passes northward in May and southward in September and October.

*345. **Turdus aonalaschkæ pallasii** (*Cab.*). HERMIT THRUSH. (759b.)—Eastern North America, breeding from northern Michigan and Massachusetts northward, and southward along the Alleghanies to Pennsylvania; winters from southern Illinois and Pennsylvania to the Gulf States. This species is an abundant migrant and occasionally is found in small numbers during the winter. In the spring it reaches us about April 10 and has passed by May 1; its fall migration takes place between October 1 and November 1. There is a record of its probable breeding at Lake Ronkonkoma, L. I. (*Dutcher*, Auk, III, 1886, p. 443).

*346. **Merula migratoria** (*Linn.*). AMERICAN ROBIN. (761.) —"Eastern North America to the Rocky Mountains, including eastern Mexico and Alaska. Breeds from near the southern border of the United States northward to the Arctic Coast; winters from southern Canada and the Northern States (irregularly) southward". The Robin is our most abundant summer resident, and in favorable localities a few may be found in the winter. Migrants begin to arrive toward the last of February and the species is abundant until December. (See Group, Gallery, between Cases A and B.)

347. **Saxicola œnanthe** (*Linn.*). WHEATEAR. (765.)— 'Europe, North Africa, Asia, Alaska, Greenland, and Labrador, straggling south to Nova Scotia, Maine, Long Island and the

Plate IV. AMERICAN ROBIN.

Bermudas." This northern species is of accidental occurrence in this vicinity; it has been twice recorded from Long Island (*Lawrence*, Ann. Lyc. Nat. Hist., VIII, 1866, p. 282; *Dutcher*, Auk, X, 1893, p. 277).

*348. **Sialia sialis** (*Linn.*). BLUEBIRD. (766.)—Eastern United States, breeding from the Gulf States to Manitoba and Nova Scotia, and wintering from southern Illinois and southern New York southward. The Bluebird is here a common summer resident, an abundant migrant, and a not infrequent winter resident. Migrants begin to arrive from the south early in March.

ERRATA.

p. 31, line 1, for Palharope read Phalarope.

p. 47, insert Family Micropodidæ.—Swifts, before No. 200, Chætura pelagica.

p. 50, line 5, for Alaada read Alauda.

p. 58, Fig. 21, for Pine Finch read Redpoll.

p. 60, Fig. 22, for Savanna Sparrow read Vesper Sparrow.

LIST OF
PRINCIPAL PAPERS RELATING TO THE BIRDS OF THE VICINITY OF NEW YORK CITY.

1844. DE KAY, J. E. Zoology of New York, or the New York Fauna; comprising detailed descriptions of all the animals hitherto observed within the State of New York, with brief notices of those occasionally found near its borders, and accompanied by appropriate illustrations. Part II, Birds. Albany: 1 Vol , 4to, pp. xii, 380, pll. col'd, 141.

    Treats of 308 species. "Though still constantly quoted – and properly to be referred to — it has ceased to be regarded as an authority" (Coues).

1844. GIRAUD, J. P., JR. The Birds of Long Island .... New York: published by Wiley & Putnam, 161 Broadway.... 1 Vol., 8vo., pp. i–xxiv, 1–397.

    Treats of 286 species, giving descriptions and extended annotations. Only 200 copies of this work are supposed to have been placed in circulation.

1866. LAWRENCE, G. N. Catalogue of Birds observed on New York, Long, and Staten Island and the adjacent parts of New Jersey. Ann. Lyc. Nat. Hist., New York, VIII, pp. 279–300.

    A partially annotated list of 327 species.

1868. ABBOTT, C. C. Catalogue of Vertebrate Animals of New Jersey. Cooke's Geology of New Jersey. Appendix E. Birds, pp. 761–798.

    An annotated list of 301 species, abounding in errors and only to be used with discrimination.

1876. BICKNELL, E. P. Field Notes at Riverdale. Forest and Stream, VI, p. 233; also pp. 133, 148, 386, 402.

    Winter and spring notes on numerous species.

1876. STEVENS, W. G. Bird arrivals on the Harlem. Forest and Stream, VI, p. 215.
: Notes on 40 species.

1877. MERRIAM, C. HART. A Review of the Birds of Connecticut with Remarks on their Habits. Trans. Conn. Acad., IV, pp. 1–165.
: A fully annotated list of 292 species.

1877. STEVENS, W. B. [Arrivals of Birds at West Farms, N. Y., during the springs of 1874, 1875, and 1876.] Forest and Stream, VIII, p. 400.
: Dates of arrival of 32 species.

1878. BENNER, F. Bird Notes from Long Island. Forest and Stream, X, pp. 174, 215.
: Notes from Astoria on a number of species.

1878. BICKNELL, E. P. Evidences of the Carolinian Fauna in the Lower Hudson Valley, Principally from Observations taken at Riverdale, N. Y. Bull. Nutt. Orn. Club[1], III, pp. 128–132.
: On 13 Carolinian species. (See also Allen, J. A. *ibid.*, pp. 149. 150.)

1878. HUYLER, A. I. Winter Birds on the Hackensack. The Country, I, p. 149.

1878. LAWRENCE, N. T. Notes on several rare Birds taken on Long Island. Forest and Stream, X, p. 235.
: Notes on 24 species.

1878. WINKLE, N. [Spring Birds at Summit, N. J.] The Country, II, p. 57.

1879. COUES, G. H. List of Birds observed in the Naval Hospital Grounds, in Brooklyn City. Bull. Nutt. Orn. Club, IV, pp. 31–33.
: Brief notes on 60 species.

1879. HERRICK, H Notes on some Birds of Chatham, N. J. Forest and Stream, XII, p. 165.

1879–80. MEARNS, E. A. A List of the Birds of the Hudson Highlands. Bull. Essex (Mass.) Inst., X, pp. 166—179;

---

[1] Bulletin of the Nuttall Ornithological Club of Cambridge, Mass. (Vols. I—VIII, 1876—1883, continued as 'The Auk' (address, C. F. Batchelder, Treas., Cambridge, Mass.).

XI, 43-52, 154-168, 189-204; XII, 11-25, 109-128; XIII, 75-93.

    The best and most complete of our local papers, treating fully of 209 species. (See also an Addendum adding 5 species. in The Auk [1], VII, 1890, pp. 55, 56; also reviews in Bull. Nutt. Orn. Club, V, 1880, p. 175; VI, 1881, p. 172.)

1879. NICHOLS, G. N. Migration of some Warblers through Summit, N. J., during the last Spring. Forest and Stream, XII, p. 464.
    Notes on 18 species.

1879. ROOSEVELT, T. Notes on some of the Birds of Oyster Bay, Long Island. One page leaflet, published by the author.
    Notes on 17 species.

1879. SCOTT, W. E. D. Late Fall and Winter Notes on some Birds Observed in the Vicinity of Princeton, N. J., 1878-79. Bull. Nutt. Orn. Club, IV, pp. 81-85.
    Notes on 35 species.

1879—85. FISHER, A. K. Occurrence of Several rare Birds near Sing Sing, N. Y. Bull. Nutt. Orn. Club, IV, pp. 61, 62.
    Notes on 5 species. For additional notes by the same author on the rarer birds of Sing Sing, see *ibid.*, III, 1878, pp. 191, 192; IV, 1879, p. 234; VI, 1881, p. 245; VII, 1882, p. 249, 251; VIII, 1883, pp. 121, 180; Auk [1], II, 1885, pp. 306, 378.

1880. LAWRENCE, R. Notes on some of the Rarer Birds of Long Island, N. Y. Bull. Nutt. Orn. Club, V, pp. 116-117.
    Notes on 8 species.

1880. STEARNS, W. A. List of Birds of Fishkill-on-Hudson, N. Y. 8vo., pp. 16. Published by the author.
    A briefly annotated list of 138 species. (Review in Bull. Nutt. Orn. Club, V, 1880, p. 233.)

1881. BERIER, DE L. Notes on a few Birds Observed at Fort Hamilton, Long Island, N. Y. Bull. Nutt. Orn. Club, VI, pp. 11-13.
    Brief notes on 10 species.

1881. BERIER, DE L. Notes on Birds Rare or Accidental on Long Island, N. Y. Bull. Nutt. Orn. Club, VI, pp. 125, 126.
    Notes on 11 species.

---

[1] The Auk, A Quarterly Journal of Ornithology. Edited by J. A. Allen. Published for the American Ornithologists' Union by L. S. Foster, 35 Pine St., New York City.

1882. TOWNSEND, A. L. [Arrival of Birds in Spring at Bay Ridge, L. I.] Forest and Stream, XVIII, pp. 305, 346, see also p. 427.
    Notes on some 30 species.

1884. BARRELL, H. F. Arrivals of Birds in [New Providence,] N. J., in 1883. Orn. and Oöl., IX, p. 45.
    A chronological list of 73 species.

1884. DUTCHER, W. Bird Notes from Long Island, N. Y. Auk, I, pp. 174-179.
    On birds striking the Fire Island and Shinnecock Bay Lighthouses.

1884-5. BICKNELL, E. P. A Study of the Singing of our Birds. Auk, I, pp. 60-71, 126-140, 209-218, 322-332; II, 1885, pp. 144-154, 249-262.
    On the song-seasons of about 100 species from observations made principally at Riverdale, N. Y.

1884--89. DUTCHER, W. Bird Notes from Long Island. Auk, I, pp. 31-35; II, 1885, pp. 36-39; III, 1886, pp. 432-444; V, 1888, pp. 169-183; VI, 1889, pp. 131-139; X, 1893, pp. 265, 266.
    A series of papers on the rarer birds of Long Island, treating of, in all, 71 species.

1885. BARRELL, H. F. Birds of the Upper Passaic Valley, New Jersey. Orn. and Oöl., X, pp. 21-23, 42, 43.
    A briefly annotated list of 149 species.

1885. HOLLICK, A. Preliminary List of the Birds known to breed on Staten Island. Proc. Nat. Sci. Assoc., Staten Island. Extra No. 4, December.
    A nominal list of 67 species.

1885. LAWRENCE, N. T. Long Island, N. Y., Bird Notes. Auk, II, pp. 272-274.
    Notes on 18 species.

1886. PAINE, A. G., JR. Dates of the Arrival of Migratory Birds in the Spring of 1886, Central Park, New York City. Orn. and Oöl., XI, pp. 109, 125.
    A chronological list of 64 species.

1886. WOODRUFF, L. B., AND PAINE, A. G., JR. Birds of Central Park, New York [City]. A Preliminary List. Forest and Stream, XXVI, pp. 386, 387; see also p. 487.
    A briefly annotated list of 121 species.

1887. THURBER, E. C. A List of Birds of Morris County, New Jersey. True Democratic Banner (newspaper), Morristown, N. J., Nov. 10, 17, 24.
: An annotated list of 205 species. (Review in Auk, V, 1888, pp.421, 422.)

1888. HALES, H. Bird Notes of Northern New Jersey. Orn. and Oöl., XIII, p. 158.
: Notes on the spring migration at Ridgewood. N. J.

1889. CHAPMAN, F. M. Notes on Birds Observed in the Vicinity of Englewood, N. J. Auk, VI, pp. 302-305.
: Notes on 19 species.

1889. CHAPMAN, F. M. Notes on the Mniotiltidæ of Englewood, N. J. Abst. Proc. Linnæan Society [No. 1], for the official year 1888-89, p. 3. (See also Auk, VI, 1889, p. 198.)
: A synopsis mentioning 8 species.

1889. CHAPMAN, F. M. Remarks on the Northern Limit of the Carolinian Fauna on the Atlantic Coast. Abst. Proc. Linnæan Society [No. 1], for the official year 1888-89, p. 4. (See also Auk, VI, 1888, p. 199.)

1889. DUTCHER, W. Long Island Birds. Forest and Stream, XXX, p. 444.
: A call for information on the occurrence of 52 species.

1889. FOSTER, L. S. Some Nyack Birds. Nyack Evening Journal, Aug. 19.

1889. LAWRENCE, G. N. An account of the Former Abundance of some species of Birds on New York Island, at the time of their Migration to the South. Abst. Proc. Linnæan Society [No. 1], for the official year 1888-89, pp. 6-8. (See also Auk, VI, 1889, pp. 201-204.)
: Notes on 13 species, from 1820 to 1850.

1890. NELSON, J. Descriptive Catalogue of the Vertebrates of New Jersey. Geological Survey of New Jersey. Final Report of the State Geologist. Vol. II, Part II. Birds, pp. 518-636.
: Based on Abbott's list of 1868 and containing numerous additional errors.

1892. AVERILL, C. K., JR. List of Birds found in the Vicinity of Bridgeport, Connecticut. Prepared for the Bridgeport Scientific Society. Bridgeport, Conn.: Buckingham & Brewer, Printers. 8vo., pp. 1-19.
: A briefly annotated list of 246 species. (See review in Auk, X, 1893, p. 352.)

1892. CHAPMAN, F. M. [Birds of Central Park, New York City.] New York Evening Post, Supplement, June 18, 25, July 2, Oct. 15, Dec. 31.
    Popular account of some species.

1892. HOWELL, A. H. Brief notes from Long Island. Auk, IX, pp. 306, 307.
    Notes on 5 species.

1893. DUTCHER, W. Notes on some Rare Birds in the Collection of the Long Island Historical Society. Auk, X, pp. 267–277.
    Notes on 44 species.

1893. EAMES, E. H. Notes from Connecticut. Auk, X, pp. 89, 90, 209.
    Notes from Bridgeport on 11 species.

1893. FOSTER, L. S. The Winter Birds of the Vicinity of New York City. Abst. Proc. Linnæan Society, No. 5, pp. 1–3.
    A synopsis mentioning 14 of a list of 127 species.

1893. HOWELL, A. H. On the Occurrence of three Rare Birds on Long Island, New York. Auk, X, 1893, pp 90, 91.
    Barn Owl, Orange-crowned Warbler, and Bicknell's Thrush.

1894. CHAPMAN, F. M. The Nocturnal Migration of Birds. Popular Science Monthly, XLV, pp. 506–511.
    Contains an account of observations made at the Statue of Liberty, Bedloe's Island.

INDEX.

Acanthis linaria, 57.
" linaria rostrata, 57.
Accidental Visitants, list of, 12.
Accipiter atricapillus, 40.
" cooperi, 40.
" velox, 40.
Actitis macularia, 36.
Ægialitis meloda, 37.
" meloda circumcincta, 37.
" semipalmata, 37.
" vocifera, 37.
" wilsoni, 37.
Agelaius phœniceus, 53.
Aix sponsa, 23.
Alauda arvensis, 50.
Alaudidæ, 50.
Alca torda, 15.
Alcedinidæ, 45.
Alcidæ, 14.
Alle alle, 15.
Ammodramus caudacutus, 60.
" caudacutus nelsoni, 61.
" caudacutus subvirgatus, 61.
" henslowi, 60.
" maritimus, 61.
" princeps, 59.
" sandwichensis savanna, 60.
" savannarum passerinus, 60.
Ampelidæ, 68.
Ampelis cedrorum, 68.
" garrulus, 68.
Anas americana, 22.
" boschas, 21.
" carolinensis, 23.
" crecca, 22.
" discors, 23.
" obscura, 22.
" penelope, 22.
" strepera, 22.
Anatidæ, 21.
Anser albifrons gambeli, 26.
Anseres, 21.
Anthus pensilvanicus, 78.

Antrostomus vociferus, 47.
Aphrizidæ, 37.
Aquila chrysaëtos, 41.
Archibuteo lagopus sancti-johannis, 41.
Ardea candidissima, 28.
" cœrulea, 28.
" egretta, 28.
" herodias, 28.
" virescens, 28.
Ardeidæ, 27.
Ardetta, 89.
Arenaria interpres, 37.
Asio accipitrinus, 43.
" wilsonianus, 43.
Auk, Razor-billed, 15.
Avocet, American, 31.
Aythya affinis, 24.
" americana, 23.
" collaris, 24.
" marila nearctica, 24.
" vallisneria, 23.

Baldpate, 22.
Bartramia longicauda, 35.
Beetle-head, 36.
Birds, Diving, 13.
" Perching, 48.
" Shore, 30.
Bittern, American, 27.
" Least, 27.
Blackbird, Crow, 54.
" Red-winged, 53.
" Rusty, 54.
Bluebird, 85.
Bobolink, 52.
Bob-white, 38.
Bonasa umbellus, 38.
Booby, 20.
Botaurus lentiginosus, 27.
Brant, 26.
" Black, 27.
Brantbird, 37.

Branta bernicla, 26.
" canadensis, 26.
" canadensis hutchinsii, 26.
" leucopsis, 27.
" nigricans, 27.
Bubo virginianus, 44.
Bubonidæ, 43.
Bufflehead, 24.
Bunting, Bay-winged, 59.
" Black-throated, 66.
" Indigo, 65.
" Painted, 65.
" Snow, 59.
Butcher-bird, 68.
Buteo borealis, 40.
" latissimus, 40
" lineatus, 40
" swainsoni, 40.
Butterball, 24.
Buzzard, Turkey, 39.

Calcarius Lapponicus, 59
" ornatus, 59.
Calico-back, 37.
Calidris arenaria, 34.
Camptolaimus labradorius, 24.
Canvasback, 23.
Caprimulgidæ, 47.
Cardinal, 65.
Cardinalis cardinalis, 65.
Carduelis carduelis, 58.
Carpodacus purpureus, 56.
Catbird, 79.
Catharista atrata, 39.
Cathartes aura, 39.
Cathartidæ, 39.
Cedar-bird, 68.
Ceophlœus pileatus, 46.
Cepphus grylle, 14.
Certhia familiaris americana, 81.
Certhiidæ, 81.
Ceryle alcyon, 45.
Chætura pelagica, 47.
Charadriidæ, 36.
Charadrius dominicus, 37.
" squatarola, 36.
Charitonetta albeola, 24.
Chat, Yellow-breasted, 77.
Chelidon erythrogaster, 67.
Chen cærulescens, 25.
" hyperborea nivalis, 25
Chewink, 65.
Chickadee, 82.
" Carolina, 82.
Chondestes grammacus, 61.
Chordeiles virginianus, 47.
Circus hudsonius, 40.
Cistothorus palustris, 81.
" stellaris, 81.
Clangula hyemalis, 24.

Chape, 46.
Clivicola riparia, 67.
Coccothraustes vespertina, 55.
Coccyges, 45.
Coccygus americanus, 45.
" erythrophthalmus, 45.
Colaptes auratus, 46.
Colinus virginianus, 38.
Columbæ, 38.
Columbidæ, 38.
Columbigallina passerina terrestris, 39.
Colymbus auritus, 13.
" holbœllii, 13.
Compsothlypis americana, 72.
Contopus borealis, 49.
" virens, 49.
Coot, American, 30.
" Black, 25.
" White-winged, 25.
Cormorant, 20.
" Double-crested, 21.
Corvidæ, 50.
Corvus americanus, 51.
" corax principalis, 51.
" ossifragus, 51.
Cowbird, 53.
Crake, Corn, 30.
Crane, 28.
Creeper, Brown, 81.
Crex crex, 30.
Crossbill, American, 56.
" White-winged, 57.
Crow, American, 51.
" Fish, 51.
Crymophilus fulicarius, 31.
Cuckoo, Black-billed, 45.
" Yellow-billed, 45.
Cuculidæ, 45.
Curlew, Eskimo, 36.
" Hudsonian, 36.
" Jack, 36.
" Long-billed, 36.
Cyanocitta cristata, 50.

Dabchick, 13.
Dafila acuta, 23.
Dendroica æstiva, 73.
" blackburniæ, 74.
" cærulea, 73.
" cærulescens, 73
" castanea, 74.
" coronata, 73.
" discolor, 75.
" dominica, 74.
" maculosa, 73.
" palmarum, 75.
" palmarum hypochrysea, 75.
" pensylvanica, 74.
" striata, 74.

Dendroica tigrina, 72.
" vigorsii, 75.
" virens, 75.
Dickcissel, 66.
Die-Dapper, 13.
Dolichonyx, 52.
Doughbird, 36.
Dove, Ground, 39.
" Mourning, 39.
Dovekie, 15.
Dowitcher, 32.
" Long-billed, 32.
Dryobates borealis, 45.
" pubescens, 45.
" villosus, 45.
Duck, American Scaup, 24.
" Black, 22.
" Crow, 30.
" Harlequin, 24.
" Labrador, 24.
" Lesser Scaup, 24.
" Raft, 24.
" Ring-necked, 24.
" Ruddy, 25.
" Rufous-crested, 23.
" Summer, 23.
" Wood, 23.
Dunlin, 34.

EAGLE, BALD, 41.
" Golden, 41.
Ectopistes migratorius, 38.
Eggs, local collection of, 3.
Egret, American, 28.
Eider, American, 25.
" King, 25.
Elanoides forficatus, 39.
Empidonax acadicus, 49.
" flaviventris, 49.
" minimus, 49.
" pusillus traillii, 49.
Ereunetes occidentalis, 34.
" pusillus, 34.
Erismatura rubida, 25.

FALCO COLUMBARIUS, 41.
" islandus, 41.
" peregrinus anatum, 41.
" rusticolus obsoletus, 41.
" sparverius, 42.
Falconidæ, 39.
Fauna, Alleghanian, southern limits of, 5.
" Carolinian, northern limits of, 5.
Finch, Grass, 59.
" Pine, 58.
" Purple, 59.
Flicker, 46.
Flycatcher, Acadian, 49.

Flycatcher, Crested, 48.
" Least, 49.
" Olive-sided, 49.
" Traill's, 49.
" Yellow-bellied, 49.
Fratercula arctica, 14.
Fringillidæ, 55.
Fulica americana, 30.
Fulmar, 19.
Fulmarus glacialis, 19.
Fute, 36.

GADWALL, 22.
Galeoscoptes carolinensis, 79.
Gallinæ, 38.
Gallinago delicata, 32.
Gallinula galeata, 30.
Gallinule, Florida, 30.
" Purple, 30.
Gannet, 20.
Gelochelidon nilotica, 17.
Geothlypis agilis, 77.
" formosa, 76.
" philadelphia, 77.
" trichas, 76.
Glaucionetta clangula americana, 24.
Gnatcatcher, Blue-gray, 83.
Godwit, Hudsonian, 34.
" Marbled, 34.
Golden-eye, American, 24.
Goldfinch, American, 57.
" European, 58
Goose, American White-fronted, 26.
" Barnacle, 27.
" Blue, 25.
" Canada, 26.
" Greater Snow, 25.
" Hutchins's, 26.
Goshawk, American, 40.
Grackle, Bronzed, 54.
" Purple, 54.
Grebe, Holbœll's, 13.
" Horned. 13.
" Pied-billed, 13.
Grosbeak, Blue, 65.
" Evening, 55.
" Pine, 55.
" Rose-breasted, 65.
Grouse, Pinnated, 38.
" Ruffed, 38.
Guara alba, 27
Guillemot, Black, 14.
Guiraca cærulea, 65.
Gull, Bonaparte's, 16.
" Burgomaster, 16.
" Glaucous, 16.
" Great Black-backed, 16.
" Herring, 16
" Kittiwake, 16.

Gull, Laughing, 16.
" Little, 17.
" Ring-billed, 16.
" Sabine's, 17.
Gyrfalcon, Black, 41.
" White, 41.

HABIA LUDOVICIANA, 65.
Hæmatopodidæ, 38.
Hæmatopus palliatus, 38.
Haliæetus leucocephalus, 70.
Harporhynchus rufus, 79.
Hawk, American Rough-legged, 41.
" American Sparrow, 42.
" Broad-winged, 40.
" Chicken, 40.
" Cooper's, 40.
" Duck, 41.
" Hen, 40.
" Marsh, 40.
" Pigeon, 41.
" Red-shouldered, 40.
" Red-tailed, 40.
" Sharp-shinned, 40.
" Swainson's, 40.
Hell-diver, 13.
Helminthophila celata, 72.
" chrysoptera, 71, 72
" lawrencei, 71.
" leucobronchialis, 71.
" peregrina, 72.
" pinus, 70.
" ruficapilla, 72.
Helmitherus vermivorus, 70.
Hen, Marsh, 29.
" Meadow, 29.
" Mud, 29.
" Prairie, 38.
Herodiones, 27.
Heron, Black-crowned Night, 28.
" Great Blue, 28.
" Green, 28.
" Little Blue, 28.
" Snowy, 28.
" Yellow-crowned Night, 28.
High-hole, 46.
Himantopus mexicanus, 31.
Hirundinidæ, 66.
Histrionicus histrionicus, 24.
Hummingbird, Ruby-throated, 47.
Hydrochelidon nigra surinamensis, 19.

IBIDIDÆ, 27.
Ibis, Glossy, 27.
" White, 27.
Icteria virens, 77.
Icteridæ, 52.
Icterus galbula, 54.
" spurius, 54.
Ionornis martinica, 30.

JAEGER, Parasitic, 15.
" Pomarine, 15.
" Long-tailed, 15.
Jay, Blue, 50.
" Canada, 50.
Junco, 63.
Junco hyemalis, 63.

KILDEER, 37.
Kingbird, 48.
" Arkansas, 48.
Kingfisher, Belted, 45.
Kinglet, Golden-crowned, 82.
" Ruby-crowned, 82.
Kite, Swallow-tailed, 39.
Kittiwake, 16.
Knot, 33.

LANIIDÆ, 68.
Lanius borealis, 68.
" ludovicianus, 68.
Lapwing, 36.
Laridæ, 16.
Lark, Horned, 50.
" Prairie Horned, 50.
" Shore, 50.
Larus argentatus smithsonianus, 16.
" atricilla, 16.
" delawarensis, 16.
" glaucus, 16.
" marinus, 16.
" minutus, 17.
" philadelphia, 16.
Limicolæ, 30.
Limosa fedoa, 34.
" hæmastica, 34.
Longipennes, 15.
Longspur, Chestnut-collared, 59.
" Lapland, 59.
Loon, 13.
" Black-throated, 14.
" Red-throated, 14.
Lophodytes cucullatus, 21.
Loxia curvirostra minor, 56.
" leucoptera, 57.

MACROCHIRES, 47.
Macrorhamphus griseus, 32.
" scolopaceus, 32.
Mallard, 21.
Marlin, Brown, 34.
" Ring-tailed, 34.
Martin, Purple, 66.
Meadowlark, 54.
Megascops asio, 44.
Melanerpes carolinus, 46.
" erythrocephalus, 46.
Melospiza fasciata, 63.
" georgiana, 64.
" lincolni, 64.

Merganser americanus, 21.
" serrator, 21.
Merganser, American, 21.
" Hooded, 21.
" Red-breasted, 21.
Merula migratoria, 84.
Micropalama himantopus, 33.
Micropodidæ, 86.
Mimus polyglottos, 79.
Mniotilta varia, 70.
Mniotiltidæ, 70.
Mockingbird, 79.
Molothrus ater. 53.
Motacillidæ, 78.
Murre, Brünnich's. 14.
Myarchus crinitus, 48.

NETTA RUFINA, 23.
Nighthawk, 47.
Numenius borealis, 36.
" hudsonicus, 36.
" longirostris, 36.
Nuthatch, Red-breasted, 81.
" White-breasted, 81.
Nyctala acadica, 44.
Nyctea nyctea, 44.
Nycticorax nycticorax nævius, 28.
" violaceus, 28.

OCEANITES OCEANICUS, 20.
Oceanodroma leucorhoa, 20.
Oidemia americana, 25.
" deglandi, 25.
" perspicillata, 25.
Old-Squaw, 24.
Old-Wife, 24.
Olor columbianus, 27.
Oriole, Baltimore, 54.
" Orchard, 54.
Osprey, American, 42.
Otocoris alpestris, 50.
" alpestris praticola, 50.
Ovenbird, 76.
Owl, American Barn, 42.
" American Long-eared, 43.
" Barred, 43.
" Great Gray, 44.
" Great Horned, 44.
" Hawk, 44.
" Saw-whet, 44.
" Screech, 44.
" Short-eared, 43.
" Snowy, 44.
Oxeye, Meadow, 33.
" Sand, 34.
Oyster-catcher, 38.

PALUDICOLÆ, 29.
Pandion haliaëtus carolinensis, 42.

Paridæ, 81.
Partridge, 38.
Parus atricapillus, 82.
" bicolor, 81.
" carolinensis, 82.
Passerella iliaca, 64.
Passer domesticus, 56.
Passeres, 48.
Passerina ciris, 65.
" cyanea, 65.
Pavoncella pugnax, 35.
Peep, 33, 34.
Pelecanidæ, 21.
Pelecanus erythrorhynchos, 21.
" fuscus, 21.
Pelican, Brown, 21.
" White, 21.
Perisoreus canadensis, 51.
Permanent Residents, list of, 7.
Petrel Leach's, 20.
" Stormy, 20.
" Wilson's, 20.
Petrochelidon lunifrons, 67.
Pewee, Wood. 49.
Phalacrocoracidæ, 20.
Phalacrocorax carbo, 20.
" dilophus, 21.
Phalarope, Northern, 31.
" Red, 30.
" Wilson's, 31.
Phalaropodidæ, 30.
Phalaropus lobatus, 31.
" tricolor, 31.
Philohela minor, 31.
Phœbe, 49.
Pici, 45.
Picidæ, 45.
Pigeon, Passenger, 38.
" Wild. 39.
Pinicola enucleator, 55.
Pintail, 23.
Pipilo erythrophthalmus, 65.
Pipit, American, 78.
Piranga erythromelas, 66.
" ludoviciana, 66.
" rubra, 66.
Plectrophenax nivalis, 59.
Plegadis autumnalis, 27.
Plover, American Golden, 37.
" Belted Piping, 37.
" Black-bellied, 36.
" Field, 35.
" Piping, 37.
" Semipalmated, 37.
" Upland, 35.
" Wilson's, 37.
Podicipidæ, 13.
Podilymbus podiceps, 13.
Polioptila cærulea, 83.

Poocætes gramineus, 59.
Porzana carolina, 29.
" jamaicensis, 29.
" noveboracensis, 29.
Procellaria pelagica, 20.
Procellariidæ, 19.
Progne subis, 66.
Protonotaria citrea, 70.
Puffin. 14.
Puffinus auduboni, 19.
" borealis, 19.
" major, 19
" stricklandi, 19.
Pygopodes, 13.

QUAIL, 38.
Quiscalus quiscula, 54.
" quiscula æneus, 54.

RAIL, Black, 29.
" Carolina, 29.
" Clapper, 29.
" King, 29.
" Virginia, 29.
" Yellow, 29.
Rallidæ, 29.
Rallus elegans, 29.
" longirostris crepitans, 29.
" virginianus, 29.
Raptores, 39.
Raven, American, 51.
Recurvirostra americana. 31.
Recurvirostridæ, 31.
Redhead, 23.
Redpoll, 57.
" Holbœll's, 57.
Redstart, American, 78.
Reedbird, 52.
Regulus calendula, 82.
" satrapa, 82.
Rissa tridactyla, 16.
Robin, American, 84.
Ruff, 35.
Rynchopidæ, 19.
Rynchops nigra, 19.

SANDERLING, 34.
Sandpiper, Baird's, 33.
" Bartramian, 35.
" Buff-breasted, 36.
" Curlew, 34.
" Least, 33.
" Pectoral, 33.
" Purple, 33.
' Red-backed, 34.
" Semipalmated, 34.
" Solitary, 35.
" Spotted, 36.
" Stilt, 33.

Sandpiper, Western, 34.
" White-rumped, 33.
Sapsucker, Yellow-bellied, 46.
Saxicola œnanthe. 84.
Sayornis phœbe, 49.
Scoleophagus carolinus, 54.
Scolopacidæ, 31.
Scolopax rusticola, 31.
Scoter, American, 23.
" Surf, 25.
" White-winged, 25.
Scotiaptex cinerea, 44.
Seiurus aurocapillus, 76.
" motacilla, 76.
" noveboracensis, 76.
" noveboracensis notabilis, 76.
Setophaga ruticilla, 78.
Shearwater, Audubon's, 19.
" Cory's, 19.
" Greater, 19.
" Sooty, 19.
Shelldrake, 21.
Shoveller, 23.
Shrike, Loggerhead, 69.
" Northern, 68.
Sialia sialis, 85.
Sickle-bill, 36.
Siskin, Pine, 58.
Sitta canadensis, 81.
" carolinensis, 81.
Skimmer, Black, 19.
Skylark, 50.
Snipe, English, 32.
" Surf, 34.
" Wilson's, 32.
Snowbird, 63.
Snowflake, 59.
Somateria dresseri, 25.
" spectabilis, 25.
Sora. 29.
South-Southerly, 24.
Sparrow, Acadian Sharp-tailed, 61.
" Chipping, 63.
" English, 56.
" Field, 63.
" Fox, 64.
" Grasshopper, 60.
" Henslow's, 60.
" House, 56.
" Ipswich, 59.
" Lark, 61.
" Lincoln's, 64.
" Nelson's, 61.
" Savanna, 60.
" Seaside, 61.
" Sharp-tailed, 60.
" Song, 63.
" Swamp, 64.
" Tree, 62.

Sparrow, Vesper, 59.
" White-crowned. 62.
" White-throated. 62.
" Yellow-winged, 60.
Spatula clypeata, 23.
Sphyrapicus varius, 46.
Spinus pinus, 58.
" tristis, 57.
Spiza americana, 66.
Spizella monticola, 62.
" pusilla, 63.
" socialis, 63.
Spoonbill, 23.
Sprigtail, 23.
Starling, 52.
Steganopodes, 20.
Stelgidopteryx serripennis, 68.
Stercorariidæ, 15.
Stercorarius longicaudus, 15.
" parasiticus, 15.
" pomarinus, 15.
Sterna antillarum, 18.
" dougalli, 18.
" forsteri, 17.
" fuliginosa, 18.
" hirundo, 17.
" maxima, 17.
" paradisæa, 18.
" tschegrava, 17.
Stilt, Black-necked, 31.
Strigidæ, 42.
Strix pratincola, 42.
Sturnella magna, 54.
Sturnidæ, 52
Sturnus vulgaris, 52.
Sula bassana, 20.
" sula, 20.
Sulidæ, 20.
Summer Residents, list of, 8.
" Visitants, list of, 9.
Surnia ulula caparoch, 44.
Swallow, Bank, 67
" Barn, 67.
" Cliff, 67.
" Rough-winged, 68.
" Sea, 17.
" Tree, 67.
Swan, Whistling, 27.
Swift, Chimney, 47.
Swimmers, Lamellirostral, 21.
" Long-winged, 15.
" Totipalmate, 20.
" Tube-nosed, 19.
Sylvania canadensis, 78.
" mitrata, 78.
" pusilla, '78.
Sylviidæ, 82.
Symphemia semipalmata, 35.
" semipalmata inorata, 35.
Syrnium nebulosum, 43.

TACHYCINETA BICOLOR, 67.
Tanager, Louisiana, 66.
" Scarlet, 66.
" Summer, 66.
Tanagridæ, 66.
Teal, Blue-winged, 23.
" European Green-winged, 22.
" Green-winged, 23.
Tern, Arctic, 18.
" Black, 19.
" Caspian, 17.
" Common, 17.
" Forster's, 17.
" Gull-billed, 17.
" Least, 18.
" Roseate, 18.
" Royal, 17.
" Sooty, 18.
Tetraonidæ, 38.
Thrasher, Brown, 79.
Thrush, Bicknell's, 84.
" Gray-cheeked, 84.
" Hermit, 84.
" Olive-backed, 84.
" Wilson's, 83.
" Wood 83.
Thryothorus ludovicianus, 79.
Tip-up, 36.
Titlark, 78.
Titmouse, Tufted, 81.
Totanus flavipes, 35.
" melanoleucus, 35.
" solitarius, 35.
Towhee, 65.
Transient Visitants, Irregular, list of, 11.
" " Regular, list of, 10.
Tringa alpina, 34.
" alpina pacifica, 34.
" bairdii, 33.
" canutus, 33.
" ferruginea, 34.
" fuscicollis, 33.
" maculata, 33.
" maritima, 33.
" minutilla, 33.
Trochilidæ, 47.
Trochilus colubris, 47.
Troglodytes aëdon, 80.
" hiemalis, 80.
Troglodytidæ, 79.
Tryngites subruficollis, 36.
Tubinares, 19.
Turdidæ, 83.
Turdus aliciæ, 84.
" aliciæ bicknelli, 84.
" aonalaschkæ pallasii, 83.
" fuscescens, 83.
" mustelinus, 83.
" ustulatus swainsonii, 84.
Turnstone, 37.

Tympanuchus cupido, 38.
Tyrannidæ, 48.
Tyrannus tyrannus, 48.
" verticalis, 48.

URIA LOMVIA, 14.
Urinator arcticus, 14.
" imber, 13.
" lumme, 14.
Urinatoridæ, 13.

VANELLUS VANELLUS, 36.
Veery, 83.
Vireo flavifrons, 69.
" gilvus, 69.
" noveboracensis, 70.
" olivaceus, 69.
" philadelphicus, 69.
" solitarius, 69.
Vireo, Black-headed, 69.
" Philadelphia, 69.
" Red-eyed, 69.
" Warbling, 69.
" White-eyed, 70.
" Yellow-throated, 69.
Vireonidæ, 69.
Vulture, Black, 39.
" Turkey, 39.

WARBLER, Bay-breasted, 74.
" Black and White, 70.
" Blackburnian, 74.
" Black-poll, 74.
" Black-throated Blue, 73.
" Black-throated Green, 75.
" Blue-winged, 70.
" Brewster's, 71.
" Canadian, 78.
" Cape May, 72.
" Cerulean, 73.
" Chestnut-sided, 74.
" Connecticut, 77.
" Golden-winged, 72.
" Hooded, 78.
" Kentucky, 76.
" Lawrence's, 71.
" Magnolia, 73.
" Mourning, 77.
" Myrtle, 73.
" Nashville, 72.
" Orange-crowned, 72.

Warbler, Palm, 75.
" Parula, 72.
" Pine, 75.
" Prairie, 75.
" Prothonotary, 70.
" Tennessee, 72.
" Wilson's, 78.
" Worm-eating, 70.
" Yellow, 73.
" Yellow-palm, 75.
" Yellow-rumped, 73.
" Yellow-throated, 74.
Water-Thrush, 76.
" Grinnell's, 76.
" Louisiana, 76.
Waxwing, Bohemian, 68.
" Cedar, 68.
Wheatear, 84.
Whip-poor-will, 47.
Whistler, 24.
Widgeon, American, 22.
" European, 22.
Willett, 35.
" Western, 35.
Winter Residents, list of, 9.
" Visitants, list of, 10.
Woodcock, American, 31.
" European, 31.
Woodpecker, Downy, 45.
" Hairy, 45.
" Pileated, 46.
" Red-bellied, 46.
" Red-cockaded, 45.
" Red-headed, 46.
" Yellow-bellied, 46.
Wren, Carolina, 79.
" House, 80.
" Long-billed, 81.
" Short-billed, 81.
" Winter, 80.

XEMA sabinii, 17.

YELLOW-LEGS, 35.
" Greater, 35.
" Summer, 35.
Yellow-throat, Maryland, 77.

ZENAIDURA MACROURA, 39.
Zonotrichia albicollis, 62.
" leucophrys, 62.

www.ingramcontent.com/pod-product-compliance
Lightning Source LLC
Chambersburg PA
CBHW030407170426
43202CB00010B/1523